Anecdotal Evidence
Stories From the Life of a Saskatchewan Veterinarian

Written by Harvey Domoslai
Edited by Ryan Domoslai
Illustrated by Joe Domoslai

Anecdotal Evidence: Stories From the Life of a Saskatchewan
Veterinarian by Harvey Domoslai
Copyright © 2020 Harvey Domoslai. All rights reserved.
Published by Harvey Domoslai ISBN 978-1-716-78886-4

Special thanks to my father Andrew for his calm guidance throughout my life. I have tried to treat animals in a kind, compassionate, manner that echoes the life he lived. Everlasting adoration for my Mother Eva who traded flowers for frogs when she chose to populate her house with seven rambunctious boys. Many thanks to my children Kyla and Ryan who allowed me to live the life of a mixed animal vet. They put up with all the absences and disruptions the lifestyle wrought on them. Special thanks to Lisa, my super supportive wife who maintained a loving home for me to rest and single-handedly attended to so many things that I should have looked after for her. Thank you to all the many clients over the years who have left me so many memories and entrusted me with their pets and/or livelihood. All your support is forever appreciated.

Thank you,
Dr. Harv

Contents

Introduction

I have been extremely blessed for my entire life and, although I have taken wrong turns, strong people around me have always steered me straight. I was a typical farm boy growing up in southern Saskatchewan on a half section of land with my dad Andrew, mother Eva, along with my six brothers. Many positive influences throughout school lead me to a degree at University of Saskatchewan and a 10 year career as a Naval Officer in the Canadian Navy. I returned to school with the support of my wife Lisa and Kyla my pre-vet kid. Ryan arrived after vet school where my vet adventures began. Dr. Doug Allen was an early career influence and took me under his wing at Park Range Vet Clinic in Prince Albert. When I returned back to Saskatoon, Dr. Wally Kononoff became a mainstay in my development as a veterinarian as my career progressed with him at Corman Park Vet Services. I started writing some of my adventures as a vet after encouragement from Shelly Sowter with the RM Review. This collection is from some of those previously published stories. I hope you enjoy them as much as I enjoyed living them.

Hunting the Plains Bison

I've had to use my dart gun quite often in the past few weeks, mostly successfully darting both tame and wild animals. The most memorable occasion was a call I got to dart a calving bison cow. Bison rarely have problems giving birth but this particular cow was trying to deliver a dead calf and only one leg and head were presented. The trailing leg was binding in the pelvis and preventing the cow from giving birth. The summer pasture where the bison roamed did not contain a handling facility and the owner requested the service of me and my dart gun. Bison do not respond very well to most common anesthetics on hand but I loaded up the truck with all that I had and proceeded to the buffalo pasture. Tony met me there shortly after noon and I jumped into his truck and started a hunting epic that would only finally end the following morning.

The cow was one of about a hundred cows, bulls and calves in a one section bushless pasture. The pasture was flat and open for the most part with an alkali bed and slough at one end with a small raised area in the center of the slough. The cow in question milled around the other animals using evolutions design to prevent her being singled out as potential prey. Tony expertly worked his old Dodge amongst the nervous beasts until I was able to fire a loaded dart at the cow's rear end. Thirty minutes later we had no effect. Again Tony maneuvered in and I fired another dart into the still alert cow. This time she started to wobble around and finally lay down an hour later with a small herd of grunting bison surrounding her. Tony inched the Dodge up to her rear end and just as I eased out to try to pull the calf out she lurched up and staggered away. The surrounding animals' defensive posturing prevented us from trying to rope her and pull her down so an hour later I darted her again. In response she slowly staggered across the alkali flat and finally lay down on the other side of the paddock by herself. We were able to drive up to her but again just as I touched the dead calf, she staggered to her feet and slowly wandered back to the main herd. She was breathing quite heavily and I was worried about the cumulative bad effects of the drugs so we decided to let her slightly recover then give her a large dose, guaranteed to work. It was around 9pm when we once again approached the now wide awake bison and I shot a massive dose of sedative into her.

This time it worked to perfection and as daylight faded we watched her stagger across the belly deep water of the slough and stretch out on the little island where she went fast asleep. It was impossible to follow on foot this time as other bison had joined her on the island and made approaching on foot dangerous. Our only option was to go home and try again in the morning.

I returned to Tony's farm early the following morning and while glassing the pasture with Tony we saw the cow at the far corner of the pasture stretched out with the dead calf still hanging from her. She was lying right against the fence so I decided to try and belly crawl up to her and possibly tie a rope to the dead calf without her knowing it. We drove around the perimeter of the pasture and stopped about a half mile away. I jumped from the truck and like Cody Robbins sneaking on a buck, I belly crawled in the ditch to within feet of her. Just as I was adjusting my calving rope to hook a foot on the dead calf she must have sensed me and with a loud grunt leaped to her feet and four legged hopped away from me. Her forceful exertion to escape from me served to wonderfully propel the dead fetus out of her which landed at my feet. The bison raced back to the herd, occasionally looking disdainfully back at me over her shoulder as if to say, "Thanks for nothing", a sentiment I echoed back to her.

Christmas Shipping Fever

It was Christmas Eve 1998 and I was home watching TV when the phone rang. A soft voice queried, "Are you Dr. Domoslai, the veterinarian?" When I answered that I was indeed, he asked me, "Are you available for a call tonight?" It was a bitterly cold night with ice fog hanging heavy in the air shrouding the darkness with its icy touch – not really the best night to be out working. The voice on the line seemed to be in need so I didn't hesitate responding, "Yes, what can I help you with?"

"Well, I've been travelling with 'some animals,'" he slowly answered. "And it seems the cold night air has caused them some trouble. They're fevered and depressed with lots of mucous coming from their noses. I can hardly get them to move!" It sounded like a classic case of shipping fever caused by stressed animals and cold weather. It wasn't unusual to get a call from a truck driver with a cattle liner full of sick calves bound for Alberta, but it was unusual to get a call like this on Christmas Eve.

"I can meet you at the office right away if you'd like," I said. "We can unload them and run them through the squeeze and doctor them there if we need to." The man answered back that that would be great and he'd be waiting for me. When I arrived at the yards, I couldn't see a semi anywhere and thought I must have arrived ahead of him. As I walked back to the squeeze area, a bearded man with grey coveralls came up to me and extended his hand saying, "Thanks for coming Doc! It sure means something for you to meet me here. I've got them all ready to go in the crowding tub. Some of them look awful sick."

"Don't worry," I reassured him. "We'll look after them."

As I stood by the cranky and cold hydraulic squeeze waiting for the first calf, I nearly dropped my jaw when into the squeeze stepped what looked like a deer of some sort. It had large antlers and a thick frost-covered hide. It stood before me caught in the squeeze with its sides wheezing in and out and ice hanging from its nostrils. Its eyes were blood shot as it dejectedly stood in front of me. "These are deer," I said to the man who stood gently scratching the sick animal. "Yes, they are," he answered. "I raise them and use them for work. They mean everything to me and look at them now. This has never happened before. They were fine before we went through Manitoba, they must have picked something up there. "

"Well they could have got sick anywhere," I responded. "But don't worry, we'll get them perked up in no time!" I took the temperature of the first deer and listened to the lungs. Its temperature was well over 105 degrees Fahrenheit and its lungs sounded hoarse and crackly. "It's a classic shipping fever pneumonia. We need to get some antibiotics, vitamins and anti-inflammatories into them. That should do the trick," I said. Each animal was treated with long acting liquamycin and then given an IV injection of an anti-inflammatory and vitamins. The IV anti-inflammatories started to work instantaneously and by the time we were finished the pen, the deer looked noticeably improved. The old man looked pleased as he handed me a note saying, "Here's my address. Can you send me a bill?"

"No problem," I responded (some people you could just trust and he looked like the honest sort of fellow who would pay his bill). "Here's another bottle of liquamycin in case they're still sick in three days. Do you need any help getting them loaded?"

"No," he replied. "I'll be fine, thank you so much for your help! See you soon!"

"Not if I see you first," I jokingly responded. Then I returned to my truck and drove home. It wasn't 'till I got back to my quiet house where my kids were safely sleeping in bed and the decorated Christmas tree was waiting for Santa's bounty, that something clicked in my head. My adult brain couldn't comprehend the possibility of the impossible until my trembling hands opened the note and I saw the mailing address that the man had given me: Mr. Clause, General Delivery, North Pole. Then I had to believe.

A Hunting We Will Go

The wind whipped my face as I raced through the woods pursuing my shadowy prey running through the dusky woods ahead of me. I knew I had one last chance to shoot before my quarry would hit the open field ahead and disappear in the gathering darkness. With speed born of desperation I surged ahead and reached a gap in the woods just as the first of the shapes whipped past the opening. Raising my gun as I stopped, I fired just as the second larger shape slipped through the opening 20 feet ahead. I heard the reassuring thwack and quickly moved to the large opening where I saw the pair streaking towards another bush ½ mile away. The large shape stumbled briefly before it entered the popular bluff and I knew that my shot had been true.

I was sheep hunting, not in the Rocky Mountains, but outside of Saskatoon and the sheep were not the big horn variety but the domestic "escapee" species. The sheep were a recently purchased ram and ewe that had run off while their new owners were loading them onto the trailer. I had been called to try to tranquilize them as their attempts to catch or coax them back had failed. The ewe was headstrong and wild and would not let anyone get closer than 100 yards before she would run off taking the usually quiet ram with her.

I arrived in the late afternoon and after a few failed approaches finally got the shot at the male. Arriving at the edge of the bluff in which the pair had entered, I was met by the sheep's owners in their truck. The owner of the land we were on noticed the lights of the truck and flashlights and came out in his truck as well, where we explained the situation. He was eager to help and told us that he would drive around to the other side of the bush and watch in case they made a break for it. We thanked him, and then proceeded on foot into the bush with our flashlights. Halfway through the darkened woods we jumped the ewe who went bounding away from us and out the other end of the bush, leaving the male who was passed out in a heap. We heard the waiting truck start up and give chase to the ewe while we commenced dragging the large ram back to the truck.

One down and one to go, but by now it was pitch black and our chances of catching the remaining ewe were slim. We were pleasantly surprised when the landowner drove towards us and said that he had got the ewe. I wondered how he could have accomplished such a feat and where the ewe was if he had indeed got her. Following the landowners truck across the open stubble, we came to a small bluff of trees to which he pointed saying, "She's in there, I shot her."

"What did you do?" I incredulously asked as the sheep owners took their flashlights into the bush. "I shot her. I think she was going to run onto the road," the landowner replied. Cries of "come quick!" got me running into the bush. In the flashlight's beam I saw the ewe. She was still alive, wide-eyed and scared. She was shot in the shoulder and hip and was sitting against a deadfall with blood dripping from her wounds. She didn't stand as I approached her and it was obvious that she was fatally wounded. I quickly euthanized her, then went back to the truck where the landowner was getting an earful from the sheep owners for his lack of regard and callous actions. Leaving the scene we were at least grateful to have the ram, who woke up healthy later that night. However, the success of his capture was tempered by the shooting of his running mate.

Cage Match with a Bull

A slight sound shifted my attention from the slide I was examining on the microscope and caused me to look up. The source of the sound was a two thousand pound, sweated up, stressed out, irate bull that stood two feet away on the other side of my desk glaring at me. I nervously looked around for an escape route in the tiny ten by ten room and wondered what on earth did I get into this time.

The bull in question was being sent to the USA to convey some good Saskatchewan genetics into a herd down there. He was long and deep and two years old. His sour disposition made him more suited for the Mid-Western ranching country than on this particular pure bred operation. Generally the bulls on this farm can be driven on foot up to the barn and cajoled by hand into the squeeze. This bull had been born elsewhere and was quite a bit more nervous as he was cautiously brought, head high into the barn.

The long barn had overhead doors at both ends. The bull squeeze was at one end next to an equipment room and the office where I had set up my microscope and paperwork. The bulls would generally leave the chute and then, as the overhead door in front of them was closed, would turn and proceed back out the door they had come in. We finally got the US bound bull into the squeeze and started processing him. We poked and prodded him, branding, tagging, bleeding and drawing samples while he stomped, snorted and glared at us from the safe confines of the squeeze. Finally we finished with him and I walked back to the small room beside the chute and plunked myself into a chair behind the desk to start examining his samples.

The boys were out front opening the gates and readying the barn for the worked-up bull's departure and the last thing I remember was the call to "Let him out!" The tiny room I was in had one door into it and one small sealed window. It was empty except for a few boxes lying around the desk I occupied, but now the bull towered above my desk and looked straight at me as I pondered my options. The door was open behind him, but in order to reach it, I would have to sneak down the side of the bull without him spinning and blocking my exit. As the low probability of success for this idea of escape bounced around in my head, the bull swung his butt a quarter turn to look out the window and, like a housewife closing the fridge with her hip, slammed the door and my only exit shut.

Now the fetal position started sounding good and I shrunk my body as small and unobtrusive as possible behind the desk and avoided eye contact. I started to weigh the odds of not getting trampled if this bull, now locked in a ten by ten room, decided to start wrecking things. Just before I was going to start to cry, the bull's owner, with good sense, pushed the door open with his show cane. The door swung inward, just brushing the bull's rear end and caused him to look over his shoulder. Seeing the door open, he spun, hip checking the desk as he went, and walked out leaving me shaking in a puddle of pee (I told the farmer the bull had peed in the room and I think he believed me).

Calving Season Warning

March is here, and with it, calving season. Every year I hear of some poor soul getting mauled by a cow that had just calved. It pays to remind ourselves of the dangers that lurk when calving cows and the care we must take to expect the unexpected. My own lesson occurred many years ago when I was a wee tadpole, but has stuck with me ever since. My father bought twenty ewes one fall when I was around twelve and we quickly befriended the quiet ones and named them according to what was obvious i.e. Baldy, Blacky, Curly, or by their steel tag numbers; #8, #21, etc. #21 was everyone's favorite and would let you scratch her behind the ear or eat out of your hand. She was always the first to come running over when the bus dropped us off and had the big brown trusting eyes that she used to parlay into extra grain or a long scratch on the itchy spots. The ewes were all bred that fall and passed an easy winter in a little pen next to the barn, a kind of hobby for us boys against the constant mucking with cattle. Sheep chores were always a breeze as one bale fed almost all the sheep and sheep didn't drink nearly as much as cattle, a fact which was much appreciated when hauling water by the bucket.

In early spring the big bulging bellies of the ewes began to bring forth lambs. As each ewe lambed we would check out the newborns and see what we had. One day after school we were told that #21 had lambed and was in a pen by herself mothering up. I was the first one to the pen and leaping over the rail fence, jumped into the pen ready to congratulate old #21 and check out her twins. I had no sooner landed on my feet in her pen and looked up when #21, my pet, my friend, head lowered at me and at full speed, rammed me in the guts. My air went out of my lungs and as I clung incredulously to the rail #21 backed up about ten steps then rammed me again this time in my hip as I turned to avoid her. Then as I breathlessly attempted to crawl over the rail fence she nailed me with her bony head square in my buttocks jamming me into the rough poplar rails and nearly disemboweling me. I toppled over the fence and stood painfully groaning beside #21's pen, while inside the ewe stood head high, stamping her feet at me seeming oblivious to any previous relationship we had. It took about four days before #21 returned to her old self although we were all careful not to get caught between her and her lambs.

After her betrayal we were never able to regain the old feelings we had had for her. It was a valuable lesson to a young fellow and I never forgot to be careful around recently freshened animals regardless of previous good behavior. My only slip up was on the direction of my wife's obstetrician when, against my better judgment, he placed me directly in a small room with my wife while she was giving birth. Thankfully I suffered only verbal abuse whose emotional scars have mostly healed.

Tick Paralysis Grips the Region

Never before in the history of mankind has a scourge, the like of what we are facing now, been experienced. Just as the biblical plague gripped and immobilized entire populations, we are once again on the brink of another catastrophe. "Oh good doctor, why be such a harbinger of doom?" you might ask me. "And what is this deadly beast that you speak of?" How could I remain silent, when I have lived it and with my own two eyes seen it in the very office where I work and also in the very house I live? The creature of which I speak is none other than the common dog tick (canus tickus teribilalis). Oh you laugh, ha, ha who would be afraid of the watermelon seed shaped wood tick? But laugh not, for I have seen the dread and despair of those stricken with these blood suckers. Grown men whimpering and fading away as the tiny ticks sucked their life's blood. Women who have spent their lives and their fortunes on their small pet dogs, literally throwing them at my feet in disgust as the dog tick, Jekyll like, turned Fifi into the most repulsive of beings. Men high stepping through the grasses with pantaloons tucked into their boots like a courtier, lest the vicious pests gain entrance onto their being. Horsemen and women have been avoiding events just because a tick was sighted in the vicinity. Don't talk to me of the harmless dog tick until you have lived the fear and survived such a vicious attack. We have had the unfortunate experience at our clinic, where dogs have come in with multiple tick attached, all simultaneously drawing blood from the poor pet. We have been able to save them all so far but not without the full weight of modern medicine and a great deal of fates good fortune. You would perhaps believe that after the tick is removed and vigilantly destroyed the problem is solved, but this little beast is not so easily removed. A small amount of blood toxin infiltrates the victim, or if it is a pet then its owner may be afflicted. This toxin circulates to the brain where it permeates such a state of paranoia that frequently immobilizes the victim ala "tick paralysis". The victim will start questioning "is the head still in?", "will it migrate to the brain and lay eggs?", "should I ever go outside again?", etc.... No wonder the paralysis. If you could only imagine the possibility of migrating ticks laying eggs in your brain even the most able minded individual would melt. No, I say to you! Beware the warm winds that have brought this deathly parasite to our once safe borders. Do not let your vigilance wane. Pet owners, do not stop in your endless search for these tiny creatures. Parents check your children and husbands, thoroughly examine your wives. Only through painstaking care and the realization that the harmless dog tick (canus tickus teribilalis), is in fact our greatest enemy do we stand a chance of survival.

Winter Survival

One of my favorite cartoons is the one where the poor frog is being swallowed by a crane. The little frog has his head already deep inside the stork's mouth, but is still valiantly trying to choke the crane with his skinny legs. Sometimes when the Saskatchewan wind blows and Mother Nature tries swallowing us up, I remember a night many years ago.

It was the middle of January and I had a call east of town to help a heifer that was trying to calve out a huge, rotten, dead calf. All of the neighbors had tried and now as bed time approached I was going to give it a go. The night was extremely cold and still, with the icy snow loudly crunching as my frozen truck creaked over the grids. The full moon shone bright over snow covered fields and as I drove hunched into my heater fighting the cold that tried to creep into my truck, I thought, "How in the world can animals survive in this extreme temperature?" I found it hard to imagine that deer, coyotes, mice and birds were out there in the dark and surviving this harshness.

I got to the farm and quickly got to work. The poor heifer was standing dejectedly tied to a post in the middle of the open shed. Her rear end was terribly swollen and I could barely reach in to feel what was going on. The situation was not that good as the large emphysematous dead calf lay with its head cocked to the side and had only the swollen feet protruding. I would not be able to pull the calf out without amputating the head, which I did. Then as we pulled on the front feet the calf pulled apart and there we stood in the straw with a head and two legs and the rest of the calf still inside the heifer. We dragged the parts away to the barn door and I got back inside of her to find that things had only gotten even tighter. I would have to take the calf out piece by piece and so rib after rib I pulled out the rotten remains, tossing the parts in a pile by the door. After about 30 minutes of painstaking tearing and pulling, I was finally able to feel over the calved hips and found that the heifer's uterus was torn. A torn uterus in a healthy cow is life threatening, but one with a dead calf inside and already in shock was always fatal. I told the farmer what I had found and he agreed that putting her down was the best thing to do.

The farmer kindly saved her the indignity of being put to sleep out in the cold and allowed me to euthanize her where she stood inside the shed. We were sadly standing around the departed cow commiserating on what a waste of a good heifer this was, when a flash of white caught our eyes. The shed door where we had piled the ribs and the parts was opened a tiny bit and a small drift of snow had been reaching at us all night. Through the crack in the door over the icy wisp of snow, a tiny lesser weasel stuck his white head and shoulders in. His black eyes were looking at us from a scant ten feet away, then he looked at the smorgasbord laid out for him. He seemed to ask, "Are you going to eat that or can I have some?" When neither of us moved he cautiously approached the pile of ribs, picked the largest of them (close to twice his size), grabbed it in his teeth and slowly backed up across the shed, up the drift and out the crack in the door... all the time looking at us like a dog with a huge Flintstones bone.

When he finally disappeared, the farmer said that maybe it wasn't such a waste after all. I thought, during the cold drive home, of a cozy winter scene tucked away in some deep badger hole where Mr. Weasel and his family shared one large rib for supper, oblivious to Mother Nature's cold fury above them.

Jake and his Old Dog

Jake was a big Alberta farm boy who had moved to Saskatchewan when his wife was transferred with her job. He had a good hand with cattle and horses so had no problem finding work with a local rancher. He had his own place and ran a few cows and horses on a nice piece of property, which I thought looked a bit like Alberta. Jake never pined for Alberta and in his big friendly way made it seem like living in Saskatchewan was the best thing that had ever happened to him. I knew things weren't always rosy with Jake, as he would occasionally share with me troubles with his wife and how hard it was to look after their little boy without family around. On one occasion while treating a sick cow, Jake had told me that things were barely holding together and that he and his wife were close to being done. He was particularly worried about his little boy Sam who was taking the frequent fights quite hard. Sam wasn't a little boy. He was a roly polly six-year-old and the spitting image of his dad. On my occasional trips to Jake's, I would see Sam walking around the yard. He'd have his mini cowboy boots on. With cap and pistol in hand, he'd be hunting imaginary villains with Jake's old dog, Boots, following with a watchful eye. Sam and Boots were inseparable as long as cattle weren't being worked. Then it was all business for Boots. His old body would go into action and fifty pounds of Australian Shepherd would go whipping in and around the flying feet of the cows according to Jake's direction.

I was particularly distressed when a couple of weeks before Christmas, Jake called. In his slow, Alberta drawl, he told me, "It's Boots. He won't come out of his bales and he's breathing awful funny. I can't bear to shoot him myself could you come over and look after him?"

"No problem, Jake. I'll be right out," I responded.

I was soon pulling into his yard to see Jake with the worst hang-dog look I had ever seen. He looked tired, beat and ready to toss in the towel on the game of life. "What's up Jake?" I genuinely asked.

"Well it's not that I didn't expect it sooner or later, but it's about the worst time possible for me. The wife's gone and left... headed back to Alberta. It's just me and Sam now." Then he added, his eyes watering up, "Sam's in the house now. He's real sad about his mom leaving and I haven't told him we've got to put Boots down."

"That's a real shame Jake," I said while thinking that some guys seem to have to bear the burden of the world. "Let's go see Boots, I'm sure he needs some attention."

Boots had hauled himself deep in a crevice of square bales. When we had finally coaxed him out, I could tell he was in real distress. He was open-mouthed breathing and his heart was pounding through his chest wall. "I think he's in heart failure. Look at how his gums are discolored," I told Jake.

"Well, do what you have to do, Doc. We'll get through alright," Jake told me. Jake was a very down to earth cowboy type, not prone to sentimentalism, but with Christmas approaching and a little boy already hurting, I thought I'd pitch a ray of hope in his direction. "I think we can help him get a little better, if you want Jake," I offered.

"I don't want him suffering and I don't want a dog that's just going to lie around. I'd rather just put him down," Jake answered.

"I think he might perk up if we can get the fluid out of his lungs to help his old heart out," I countered.

"Well I guess it can't hurt," Jake replied. "Maybe it'll help little Sam if we keep Boots going for a while longer."

"Well, we'll give it a try. I sure hope we can help him out," I said. "Now, give me a hand getting him into the house."

Old Boots had spent his entire life living outside at the mercy of the weather. Now, the medicine, the warmth of the house and the constant presence of Sam did wonders for him. Sam was instantly out of his funk. The chance to have his old pal in the house with him through Christmas holidays was a gift in itself. Within a matter of days, the medication and house rest took effect. Boots started improving and was soon his old self. He followed Sam from room to room, letting the little guy pretend to ride him while shooting at the furniture with his six gun.

I called Jake after Christmas. He said that it had been a sad Christmas without Sam's mom but having the dog in the house eased the pain and kept Sam occupied. It had also been good for Jake. His old dog was still with him and had been someone to talk to after Sam had gone to sleep and the house felt particularly empty. Boots went on to live for two more months before he died in his sleep. Jake soon sold his place and his cows, and moved closer to his ex-wife in Alberta. The last I heard was that the little guy got a new dog and Jake's got a new wife. Life is once again as it should be for Jake and Sam.

New Winter Coat

It was a bright winter afternoon and my boy Ryan and I were hanging around at home when the phone rang. It was Reg and he had a sick calf that needed tending to. Reg lived in town but had his cows out in the bush amongst some old rundown buildings. I told him that we'd be right out. Ryan and I dressed quickly and started off to the farm.

Ryan had a brand new winter coat that his mother had warned him not to get dirty. Being a conscientious little five-year-old, he asked me a few times on the way to Reg's if we would be doing a dirty job. He reminded me that he wasn't allowed to get his coat dirty. I told him not to worry, today's job was a nice clean one and nobody was going to get dirty – especially him with his new coat. When we arrived at the farm, Reg had the little two month old beef calf tied to a post with a halter. The calf had a huge bloated stomach from a previous engorgement on alfalfa. He stood looking for help with his head hanging down dejectedly. I told Reg we'd have to tube off some of the gas then drench the calf. I positioned Ryan a few yards off out of harm's way. I mixed up the drench, which consisted of mineral oil, green pepperminty bloat-eze and cow brand baking soda and passed a tube to let off some gas.

The calf was very uncomfortable with the tube down his throat and tossed his head to and fro as I tried to find the large gas pocket to relieve his pain. After 5 – 10 minutes I had only succeeded in letting off a small amount of air and the calf looked just as bad as when I had started. I decided to drench him in the hope that that might settle things and let me take some air off. I quickly pumped the half-gallon of liquid down and then asked Reg to hold the end of the tube as I simultaneously manipulated the hose in the calf's throat and palpated his rumen. After a few more minutes we finally hit the sweet spot and she blew like Old Faithful. As Reg directed the hose away from him, all the pent up gas in the calf's belly mixed with the drench and sour rumen fluid erupted and spouted out the end of the hose. Unfortunately, Reg did not realize where the hose was and the full explosive dose of rumen concoction hit Ryan square on his shiny new winter coat. Ryan looked at his coat, then at me, tears welling up in his eyes. As he slowly backed away from the crime scene, I quickly tried to reassure him but as I wiped his coat with straw and saw that neither the stink nor the oil stain was going away, I realized that we were in trouble.

On the way home, I finally got Ryan settled down and convinced him that things got dirty when you were working with cows and it was no big deal. We'd just quietly throw his coat in the wash and Mom would be none the wiser. Ryan seemed to like the idea and I thought that we'd had a good bonding moment i.e. man and boy working together to learn how to deal with potentially irate women. This lesson quickly left Ryan as soon as we got home. The burden of guilt overcame him at the door when the smell of his Mom's cooking met him. He immediately rushed to his mother's side, dirty coat in hand exclaiming, "Daddy took me on a farm call and made this calf throw up all over my new coat and I told him not to do it!" And there I was without defense, the smelly, dirty, once brand-new coat providing all the incriminating evidence a five-year-old needed.

Castrations a la Mode

As a veterinary student working in Alberta one summer I got the chance to go on a call with Rick to castrate some grass calves for a local bachelor named Felix. On the way out to the call Rick explained to me how he had been doing the job for many years. It had become a ritual to castrate in the morning and then Felix's aged mother, whom Felix lived with, would fix up lunch and her famous Saskatoon berry pie. This year was to be different as Felix's mom had unfortunately passed away. We got to the farm and after introductions Rick, Felix, his neighbor and I started working. The neighbor brought the 700-pound bulls up the squeeze and Felix caught them, then applied a tail jack while Rick and I castrated and needled each calf. The calves had already been on pasture and were very loose and we were soon covered in processed grass.

Felix rarely said a word but very efficiently held the tails and directed most of the fecal flow away from us as we worked. After completing the job and ensuring none of the calves were still bleeding, the vet and I carefully washed our hands at the truck where Felix approached us and asked us to come up to the house for something to eat. We gladly followed him looking forward to lunch after a long morning of work. When we got to the house it became obvious that his mother had been the major force in his domestic life. Without her the house was a mess. The sink was piled deep with dirty dishes and the table was three layers deep with newspaper, bottles and laundry. Felix quickly cleared the table then asked if we wanted something to drink. Being quite thirsty we all said that we would like something to drink, whereby Felix grabbed a 26 ounce bottle of Scotch from the floor and four cups from the dirty pile in the sink and poured a good stiff 2 ounce shot for each of us. My cup had a few floaters in it and possibly a pickled fly and I thought that by careful sipping I could strain out the debris from the drink. Unfortunately, the tradition was to down the drink in a gulp and as everyone else quickly drained their shot I had to follow and choked it down chunks and all. Next Felix asked if we wanted pie, which we all agreed to have. He pulled a large 10-inch deep dish Saskatoon berry pie from the fridge and plunked it in the middle of the table. He grabbed a knife and cut the pie into four saying he had bought it at the Church bake sale. He loaded the large pieces on four dinner plates and asked if we wanted ice cream with it. Everyone agreed and he went to his porch and took out a gallon of vanilla ice cream. The deep freeze must have been working quite well as the ice cream was rock hard and after quickly bending a tablespoon Felix dug out a teaspoon and proceeded to scrape the ice cream surface and with his fingers place the slivers of ice cream on our pie. The affair was quite strenuous for Felix but by holding the spoon close to the end he was able to eventually dig out enough ice cream for all of our pies. As Felix slid the plates to the center of the table and told us to help ourselves we realized that Felix hadn't washed his hands after castrating and that what had started out as vanilla now looked more like butterscotch swirl. It was then that I appreciated the numbing significance of the shot of Scotch as we all dug into some of the best pie and ice cream I have ever had.

Shooting the Smiths' Quarter Horse

A veterinarian is daily faced with decisions that mean life or death for his patients. A cow that is diagnosed unbred after a 20-second preg check is destined for slaughter, as is a bull that fails his semen evaluation. Diagnoses on small animals often lead the owner to euthanize their favorite family pets. As a veterinarian you always hope you have done your job to the best of your abilities and have pointed your clients in the right direction. One of the most stressful situations I have experienced was some years ago when I was called to look at Jim Smith's prize quarter horse stud, Sunshine. Jim's stud was only 9 years old and was off a good line of reining horses. His offspring to date showed great promise and Jim was fetching good stud fees off him. Jim was an accountant in town and called me from work to ask me to go to his place and check Sunshine who didn't look right that morning. Jim couldn't leave work so I went to his farm and met his son who stood by the stud pen watching Sunshine. Sunshine was a beautiful well-muscled chestnut stud. Today he looked a shadow of his previous self. He was in obvious distress. His body was sweat wracked and covered in dirt and he trembled as he approached. As I watched him, he forcibly dropped to the ground and rolled over, kicking in the air as he lay on his back. We put a halter on him and after a thorough examination, I felt certain he had a severely twisted bowel. I went to the truck and called Jim to tell him what I had found. I added that additional tests could confirm the diagnosis, but would entail a two-hour trip to the Vet College. Jim then asked if it was in fact, a twisted bowel that Sunshine had, what his options were. I told him that with the severity of the signs I was seeing, the only option was a surgery with a poor prognosis for survival. I expected Jim to likely get a second opinion at the college given the value of the horse but he caught me off guard when he told me to go ahead and put him down. At this point I was a little taken back and realized that my decision had better be right or this horse was going to die regardless. I then asked Jim if I could try a dose of a potent pain reliever, which if it worked would maybe give Sunshine a more favorable prognosis. By doing this I could reassess the horse in a few hours and thereby make absolutely certain that my diagnosis was correct. Jim agreed to this and asked me to call him as soon as I made my reassessment in two hours. I gave Sunshine his medication then left to another call telling Jim's son to watch Sunshine and call me with any change. As I drove off, I quickly called my boss and described in detail what I had found. He didn't have time to personally look at the horse but assured me to do what I thought was right. Here I was a relatively inexperienced vet with an expensive horse that I had diagnosed with a severely twisted stomach. The horse's only chance of survival was through surgery and Jim had already refused that based on my poor prognosis. I knew that my diagnosis had better be right.

When I returned in two hours nothing had changed and Sunshine was in fact marginally worse. I called Jim and updated him and told him that if he wanted to have a chance to save Sunshine we needed to get him to the Vet College ASAP. Jim quietly and sadly responded that he didn't want to subject Sunshine to the surgery and couldn't bear to see his horse suffer. He asked if I could put him down and that he'd be right out if I could wait and do a post-mortem when he arrived.

There was no hiding now. The final examination was on and the only way of finding out the answer was to put the horse down. I felt as sure as I could about my decision, but a nagging doubt fueled by a fatalistic optimism lingered in my mind as I euthanized Sunshine. Jim arrived shortly after and I left him alone by his horse while I prepared my post-mortem knife. Within minutes all would be revealed and as my first incision cut through Sunshine's abdomen - my anticipation was great. As I entered the abdomen great billowing black and blue ruptured bowels rolled out of the incision gloriously confirming my diagnosis and setting my mind finally to rest. Jim's mind must have also eased as I saw the tension release from his body as he looked at the damaged bowel and knowingly nodded to me.

Sunshine on a Black Season

With the lousy weather, closed border (due to BSE), and a short summer it's been easy to get depressed. For me, whenever things get bad I think back to old Zigor, a farmer I used to know. Zigor was about sixty-five when I first met him. He had a small farm and raised about fifty polled Hereford cows. His farm was carved out of the woods and where the farms around him had pushed the forest back, Zigor's holdings remained the same as they had since his dad had first cleared the land. A collection of old run-down buildings were nestled amongst the trees and surrounded on three sides by wooded pastures into which his cows grazed.

Zigor's luck was bad and his feature and disposition reflected this: He would talk to you in a slow Ukrainian drawl laced with depression. "I tink ve need preg check now all grass gone, mayby sell all damn cows."

His one and only bright spot was his only son who was away at University studying 'to be a smart farmer'. "I only dumb farmer, Nick when he come back he do tings better," Zigor would proudly boast. I only met Nick once and he seemed to be a normal young guy, home for the weekend to help on the farm. I was quite surprised when I found out that he committed suicide just before his third year of University. I wondered and worried about how old Zigor was making out with the loss, but didn't have a chance to talk to him about it.

The year had been poor, we didn't get enough rain until it was combining time and now it was October with some crops still out and cool wet weather forecasted. Zigor called me on the phone at about 4 a.m. and said, "You come out, I got trouble wit' one kind of heifer with too big calf."

Whenever I drove into his yard I always felt like I was driving back to a different century and this October night was no different. It was frosty and damp as Zigor waved me to the corral with his flashlight.

A young heifer lay in the corner of an old wood corral with steam rising off her as she strained ineffectually to deliver her calf. I snuck up behind her and quickly determined that this was one teenage pregnancy that needed a C-section. I told Zigor and for a moment he never moved, but just stared back at me like I had dropped another load onto his back that he just couldn't bear up too. Then he asked, "Okay vat ve do now?" I told him that if we got her over to the small lean-to, we would be out of the damp. And if we rigged up a light we should be fine to do the surgery right there. The lean-to was quite cozy and between the three of us and the naked light bulb we finally had a live good looking calf on the ground. The sun was just cracking in from the east and sending nice beams through the large trees and into the lean-to as I finished suturing the heifer. I had been waiting to ask Zigor about his boy, but the time didn't seem right between talking crops and cattle. As I laid my last suture into the heifers side, I looked at Zigor and said that I was sorry to hear about his son's death. As soon as I said it, Zigor's face blackened and his hands dropped to his side. I felt again that I had dealt him a deadly blow and was sorry I had done so. Zigor then straightened up and looked me square in the eyes saying, "Maybe now ve get veat combined if weather stay nice." I knew that without answering Zigor had answered me. From the depths of his depression, I could see that the toughness of his spirit had indeed survived and like the sun's rays reaching through the forest, his spirit also sent forth a thin ray of optimism for the future.

A Good Night's Sleep

One of the drawbacks or bonuses, depending on how you look at it, of being a veterinarian is that you get to go out and about legally at all hours of the night. The nice thing is that I've seen some of the greatest sunrises and Northern Light shows and the bad thing is that a fellow gets quite tired after a while. After one particular long stretch of sleep deprivation I returned home early one evening and was looking forward to flopping in my bed and grabbing some sleep when the phone rang. It was a new customer who had just bought a new Bichon-Poodle cross pup. The pup had apparently been doing fine and quite suddenly after supper started crying painfully and now had a swollen belly. I told the concerned owner that I would meet her at the clinic right away and see what I could do.

The little pup was about ten weeks old and as cute as a button as he huddled in the arms of his owner, whimpering painfully. He had a much-enlarged abdomen but even so was friendly and started to lick my hand as I examined him. After a thorough going over, I determined that we should open him up as I suspected a torsion of the stomach. I informed the customer of what I thought we should do and that she should leave the pup overnight. I would get back to her after I was completed.

I called one of the vet techs in to assist me and then proceeded with the surgery. As I suspected, the stomach was twisted but due to the acute nature of the twist it was easily and (I thought) successfully repaired. We finished cleaning up around 11 PM and after I called the owner and gave her the good news I got ready to leave the clinic. Checking on the pup one last time I found him a bit cold and breathing irregularly as he recovered from surgery. I decided to take the pup home instead of leaving him alone overnight at the clinic. I said goodnight to the tech and told her I'd see her bright and early in the morning.

By the time I got home the pup's breathing had stabilized although he continued to sleep soundly under the influence of the anesthetic. I fashioned a small box into a dog bed and placed a hot water bottle and a towel in it and set it on the floor by my bed, hoping that I would get a good night's sleep without any additional vet calls.

The next thing I knew the sun was shining through my window and onto my bed. Now, the sun shining in the window isn't a bad thing but I was living in a basement suite and the sun didn't rise enough to hit my bed until around noon. I jumped out of bed and stepped into a pint of dog urine. There looking at me was the little pup sitting like the king of the world in his home-made dog bed chewing nonchalantly on the severed end of the phone line with the alarm clock cord unplugged from the wall and safely stowed under him like spoor from a successful hunt. And could you believe it, when I got to the clinic, totally refreshed after my 12 hour nap and 5 hours late for work, nobody believed my story.

Jacob's Barn

March has arrived and my surgery knife was sharpened for another round of caesarean sections and fetotomys. I've conducted C-Sections on cows in many different situations from set ups that would rival city hospitals for cleanliness, to surgeries literally at the end of a rope in the middle of a field. Jacob's barn was at the far end of the bad scale. Jacob was an old country farmer who ran about fifty Hereford-cross cows. His farm was only six miles from town but it was buried in the bush. Poplar tree corrals surrounded his cabin 'barn', a squad mud building about 20X20, studded with straw and lumber. Inside, the mud and straw roof was barely seven feet high and even at my challenged height I felt like bending my head whenever I walked in. Jacob had four small pens inside the barn and usually had it well bedded for his cabin cows.

One year, Jacob bought ten bred heifers that gave him bad luck right off the get go. His first heifer was still down after a hard pull on a large dead calf. Heifer number two and three calved alright but then the fourth heifer started trying to calf a monster of a calf. Jacob called my colleague Pete at about 8 in the evening. The air was cold outside as he stepped into the welcoming warmth of the barn to find it crowded with two cows, Jacob, his two boys and a couple of spectators. He elbowed his way to the heifer and carefully palpated her. The calf was obviously not coming out without a C-Section so he rigged up lights and tied the heifer and positioned everyone to help get the calf out. Typically we would open the cow's side and present the calf's feet to a gloved assistant who attaches chains to pull the calf out of the cow's side. All had gone well and all the chains were attached to the calf by Jacob's son when Pete gave the order to pull. Jacob, taking command of the situation and eager to get his calf out of the heifer, jumped in and lent his hands to the task along with his other son and the spectators. Before Pete realized it, the five of them had pulled so hard that they toppled the heifer over on her side with the calf half out and half in. The heifer lay on her side with the little opened–eye calf squished under her looking around at his welcome committee with his legs still stuck in his mom's side. They half rolled the heifer back and Jacob and the crew finished pulling the calf out along with, much to Pete's horror, half of her intestines. There they sat a large puddle of steaming, twisted bowels lying in the dirty old barn floor while the heifer sat and mooed longingly for her newborn calf. Pete washed off the bowels as best he could but the dirt and grime had embedded into the fatty tissue and he didn't feel very optimistic about her chances. He sewed her up anyway, loaded her up on antibiotics and left her with a prayer.

Two days later when Jacob was called, she was doing great. Jacob said that he always kept his barn clean and that he knew she would be okay.

Two days later I had an opportunity to try out Jacob's surgical suite. Another heifer was calving a large calf and needed a c-section. This time I assigned one of Jacob's boys to pull the calf out and told Jacob he was to support the heifer's hips to prevent her from falling over. Jacob and his boys eagerly complied and we soon had a healthy calf on the ground. I was quite satisfied with myself this time and things were going well when I noticed that above me, the warm March wind coupled with the bodies in the barn was defrosting the dirt roof. Large drops of water carrying centuries of old dirt and bacteria now hung above the open surgical site. I tried desperately to close the site before the ancient roof let loose its centuries old toxins, but all was in vain. Two large brown drops slowly and directly landed on the cow's open abdomen as if put there by an invisible hand with an eyedropper. I did not feel that I had greatly compromised the surgery, especially compared to what Pete had gone through with the last one, but just in case, I filled her with antibiotics and cautioned Jacob to watch her in case she got sick. Jacob scoffed at my worry reminding me again of his clean barn.

Three days later when Jacob called me I knew that things were bad. The heifer was off feed, depressed and not caring for her calf. We put her on the best drugs we had but whatever was in the medieval drops of condensation couldn't be cured and the heifer died a week later full of infection. When I tried to explain to Jacob what had transpired scientifically, I found that I couldn't. The series of events went right in the face of what we had seen and expected, and all I could tell Jacob was that I didn't know why things happened like they had – just that sometimes they do.

Watching the Frog Jump

I read once in an old Andy Russel book that "you never know how far a frog might jump unless you sit down and watch him awhile". I have used this analogy to raise kids, work with staff and gauge the ability of a sick or injured animal to recover. The thing is... you never know what kind of gumption or ambition something has until you "set down and watch them awhile".

Mandy was an example of a horse that I initially thought wouldn't have the fortitude to survive the ordeal she was about to face, but somehow she did. She was a wild, little sorrel mare, with what the owners thought was a sliver in her neck. I could hardly get a hand on her as the ill-mannered mare skittered away from me, lifting her front legs and laying her ears back as I tried to get a closer look. The wound at mid-withers drained yellow chunky pus and immediately smacked to me of a fistulous withers. A fistulous withers is a deep seated infection in the bursal sacs of the wither bones that boils and bubbles chronically like porridge as the infection eats away at the muscles of the neck. A fistulous withers is a nightmare to treat in a quiet horse and even more so in a recalcitrant one. I told Mandy's owners what I thought was going on and explained the treatment process and prognosis. They were noticeably agitated. I'm sure that they were thinking that I had "fed them the goods" having shown up with a horse with a sliver in the neck and leaving with a horse that had a necrotizing and potentially fatal illness.

Initially Mandy's owners didn't agree with my diagnosis, but after two weeks of oral antibiotics and the occasional hosing down, they realized that things were getting worse. Mandy was getting sicker by the day and no easier to treat. Mandy was their daughter's only horse and had a special bond with the girl, but was proving to be too much to handle. I told her owners that I could take her to the clinic for the next month or so and attempt to clean the infection up with aggressive surgery and medications. A whole lot would depend on Mandy and if she could direct her energy towards fighting this disease rather than fighting us.

They agreed and we started down a very long and painful treatment regime. Initially, Mandy had to be sedated so that we could work on her, but eventually she caught on that we were helping her and submitted to our ministrations. Three times, large areas of her withers, muscle, ligament, and bone were removed and scraped in an attempt to eliminate the pathogen. The area would appear healed up and just as optimism returned another draining, pussing lesion would show up. Finally, six weeks later, after the fourth surgery we beat it!

Throughout this time Mandy's true colors gradually showed through. Gone was the temperamental mare we started with, now Mandy would stand quietly as we explored and debrided her wounds. She always had a friendly nicker as you approached and her redirected energy sped her recovery.

I have seen far less painful procedures sour a horse, but in Mandy's case her strength and character were surprisingly revealed in fine form. Mandy has remained fistula free for four years now and continues to be a wonderful horse.

Getting a Bucket of Warm Water

One day in the first few months as a recently graduated veterinarian, I was discussing with my boss how to sedate a misbehaving horse. I had had a great deal of trouble trying to sedate a horse in order to castrate it and was looking for some tricks of the trade. The horse in question danced and reared making it extremely difficult to get a needle in. The young owner was no help as she patted and gently admonished the horse to 'stand still' 'cause it won't hurt a bit. My boss looked down at me and said in his slow Saskatchewan drawl, "sometimes it's not the horse that needs sedation'… it's the owner. What I do in that situation is send the owner to the house to get a bucket of warm water and then when they're gone, kapow!! You give that horse a hard lesson and he'll stand nice for you." Well, I had never had the opportunity or the will to send my customers to the house so I could tune in their horses with a club, but I sure had plenty of times when I wished I could.

Not long ago, I was at John Epps, and old time horse trainer, to castrate one of his two year olds. Most of the time, the horses at his place were well trained and in his strong and rope gnarled hands completely in his control. This time, the wind was up and this horse was in no mood for a surgery on his privates. He bucked, pulled, and reared much to the consternation of his handler, who apologized as we tried every trick in the book to get him to stand still for his intravenous sedation. Finally after fifteen minutes in a losing battle with the horse picking up steam, we were losing. John turned to me and asked if I had an extra rope in my truck to help tie him up. I surely did and walked around the barn to get the rope from my truck. When I returned John stood by our patient, who now stood by his side like an attentive dog waiting for his next command. "Why don't you try the needle now Doc," old John said, presenting the now calm horse's neck to me. I gently approached and the horse never flinched as I injected him with his sedation. As the horse slowly lay down under the influence of the drugs, I noticed first a trickle of blood from his nose and then the fencepost leaning against the fence where it hadn't been before. I quickly put two and two together and realized that I had just been "sent to the house for a bucket of warm water".

Oxytetracycline the Heavenly Nectar

Oxytetracycline…street names: Liquamycin, LA, black gold, speed fix, Oxy, magic bullet, miracle gold…the names go on for this most versatile and affordable drug. LA unpretentiously sits, shielded from the sun in its big brown bottle, a simple compound of 200 milligrams of Oxytetracycline powder suspended in an oily matrix. To the uninitiated, one would see an innocuous looking enough liquid, absent of frog legs and magic fairy dust. But in this apparently mild mannered bottle lays a mythical genie, a veritable sleeping giant that beckons to be summoned for battle. Legends and folklore abounds its magical properties and heroic victories. LA was there to treat Hannibal's fevered elephants while going through the Khyber Pass. It saved Lassie when he contracted a septic bowel and nearly died and it was used extensively in Hollywood to keep the badly injured Wiley Coyote on the job. Paul Bunyan was said to have hauled it in by the train load to treat his old steer Blue's raging pneumonia and even Old Yeller was given a shot, but rabies is the one thing that LA won't touch. I myself have unabashedly used Liquamycin throughout my career, where it has stood me in good stead and got me through some mighty rough times where the other more worldly products have let me down. Now I won't say that LA in itself will cure the world's woes but in conjunction with sound judgment and experience tempered by age it has been a true blessing to my practice of veterinary medicine.

One such occasion was on a late summer call to a failing bull. The animal in question was a three year old Charolais bull in what was supposed to be the prime of his life. He had all the green grass he could eat, all the blue sky he could ponder and forty of the prettiest cows you'd ever want to spend the summer with. Despite that, he wasn't looking like he was having very much fun.

He sat slumped in the chute as I approached his whipped dog hide and started my examination. This was a once prize bull that had lost a good four hundred pounds in the last month or so and the owner was justifiably nervous. I put on my best diagnostician look and started in on him; listening, prodding, thumping and sticking my hand up where it should have never gone. I bled him, scratched him, poked his teeth and even tested his pee. When thirty minutes of intense study didn't get me any closer to an answer, I even tried sucking on a piece of grass to see if that would stimulate something in my brain that would tell me what to do. Whenever I'm backed into a corner, the farmer's glaring me down, and I've got nowhere to go, I reach for my Liquamycin. "I think he needs a good shot of LA," I said and strolled to my truck to load up a syringe. I grabbed the bottle of LA and returned to the passive bull. Reaching through the chute, I blasted 30 ccs into his neck muscle.

LA is just like Buckley's cough medicine, 'it tastes awful but it works'. LA works but it bites like a snake. When I injected that bull he opened his mouth and with tongue fully extended, let out the longest most painful fog horned bawl I have ever heard. It was then that I saw, way back over the top of his tongue (the one spot I had not checked), three porcupine quills. I went back to my truck and grabbed a set of forceps and this time when the farmer injected another 30 ccs into his neck, I quickly plucked the offending quills out as the bull again bellowed his protest. "That should do it," I quietly said and reverently laid my sweet LA down in her own special place in my medicine kit.

Green Rodents

I had a strange call last week from an out of town gentleman about his pet rodent. I don't get many calls about rodents, but I have done some work on rats, mice and the occasional ferret. So I guess I was as well qualified as anyone to answer his questions. He didn't tell me his name, which isn't uncommon in the prairies, where pets you can ride or eat are more the norm then seeking medical help for a rodent. It seems like his little pet wasn't eating much, was listless and was passing foul smelling, greenish diarrhea. It seems that his pet had a similar episode last winter which hit him hard in late November and didn't clear up till Christmas.

I asked him a few questions, then invited him to bring his pet to the clinic for a checkup. The client replied that he didn't feel comfortable bringing him as his pet loved to stick its head out of the window and was quite stressed when he couldn't see his surroundings. He didn't want to give it a chill and wondered if he could just pick up some medicine. I told him I understood and agreed to call in a prescription for some antibiotics.

Last Friday I heard from him again. He said his pet was taking his medicine if he mixed it with flaked cereal and appeared to be improving. On Monday morning, however, my phone rang again concerning my little rodent patient. It seems that since Saturday night he had taken a turn for the worse and now was stretched out near comatose. This time, I insisted the owner bring him in. Imagine my surprise, when into the Corman Park Clinic parking lot drives the Gainer the Gopher Touchdown truck. Jim Hopson jumps out of it and begins trying to entice Gainer out of his hole on the back of the truck with a head of lettuce. "Mr. Hopson," I say, "your pet rodent is actually Gainer the Gopher."

"Yes," he replied. "Most vets won't deal with him 'cause of his size and I kind of want to keep his sickness quiet so fans won't be upset." After getting Gainer out of his hole, we moved him into the clinic and gave him a complete examination. I determined that he had a severe case of stress diarrhea leading to constipation, obstipation and confiscation of pride. I told Jim that the best thing for him would be to place him into an induced coma and wake him in December after the Grey Cup. Jim told me that that was impossible as Gainer was needed to rally the flagging Rider Nation. He asked me if there was anything that could help Gainer deal with the stress of being a Rider Fan and Mascot. He was especially fearful of the upcoming back to back games against Winnipeg and was worried that losses there could put Gainer over the deep end. The only remedy I could think of would be something to dull the anxiety of failure and soothe the dagger of defeat. I couldn't put him on straight Rye whiskey, which is my own elixir for Rider losses, so I put Gainer on daily Valium and Amitriptyline, both potent anti-depressants, which I hope will help Gainer survive the season.

As of posting this story, Gainer is improving and holding food down. The true test will come this Labor Day Weekend in Regina.

I'll be watching....

Taunte's Inferno

I first met Taunte when he was just a young, full of life pup. He had an ear infection, as most sloppy golden labs that drink out of toilet bowls get. I got to know Taunte real well throughout his many ear infections and miscellaneous ailments and he was always the most patient loveable lug of a dog.

Taunte's owners were newly married and lived in a small inner city house along with numerous aunties and kids who shared their home. Taunte loved the action and the comings and goings at the house. He was a dominant force in the tiny home, ready to greet and lick you as soon as you entered. I would occasionally drop in to check on Taunte or drop off meds if he needed them. We would, invariably, move over the many kids on the floor and go to the back yard where we could sit and poke at Taunte without distractions. I would occasionally ask if they were worried about the neighborhood they lived in with all the crime that surrounded them. Taunte's owners quickly asserted that they had never had a problem and that Taunte was quite a guard dog. They felt totally protected with him around. As a goofy Taunte lie on his back and let me scratch his belly I had a hard time imagining him being an aggressive guard dog. A month ago I was proven wrong and Taunte's worth was proven.

It seems that on the September long weekend Taunte's owners left for Alberta and left the house and Taunte under the care of one of their aunts. It was around midnight on Saturday night when I got a panicked call from Taunte's owner's mother, "Taunte's been stabbed. There's blood everywhere and the police are here. I don't know what to do!" I quickly got her to calm down and asked her to check Taunte's breathing and gum color. She came back on the phone after a few minutes and told me, "don't worry, he just died." Then, she hung up leaving me wondering what had just happened.

It wasn't until later the next week that I finally spoke to Taunte's owners and found out the story. Late Saturday evening, while their aunt was alone watching TV, her estranged husband knocked on the door. He was drunk and forced himself into the house uninvited. The aunt tried to humor him, but the situation quickly turned ugly when the drunkard couldn't find any booze in the house. In a rage he grabbed a kitchen knife and violently approached his ex-wife threatening to kill her. Taunte stood protectively in front of the aunt and as the man approached, he growled a warning and jumped at him as his knife flashed toward the aunt. The startled man was temporarily stopped allowing the terrified aunt to race out the front door. The foiled drunk then turned his rage on Taunte and savagely stabbed him in the chest and neck numerous times before fleeing.

The police quickly responded to the aunt's 911 call and arrested the assailant, who was still in the neighborhood. Unfortunately for Taunte he passed away that night, a loveable yellow lab laying his life down while trying to help.

Bad Luck

The cow laid down on a Saturday in February and when she didn't get up by the next day Frank called me. "Could you come out and check her out Doc, she's a good cow. I bred her to calf early next week and I don't want to lose her," Frank drawled on the phone. I was soon at his place and after a quick exam found that she was chock full of calf and couldn't use her back legs at all. Her milk was starting to come in so my best guess was milk fever. I IV'd a couple of bottles into her and was off, sure she would be up by the next day. Frank called back the next morning, "She's still not up Doc, could you come out and check her out Doc, she's a good cow and I don't want to lose her." So once again, I was off.

After another examination we determined that the calf I could feel rectally was small. She was a huge bellied cow so we thought it was quite probable that she had twins. "Well Frank," I explained, "If she has twins, she likely won't get up now till she calves. The calves take too much energy out of her and we can't get her back 'til she calves... and even then she might not get up."

"Well Doc, like I say I don't want to lose the cow. Why don't we kick the calves out and see what happens." With that, I injected her with the proper medications to induce calving.

"She should calve in about a day and a half but watch her close because she could go at any time." A day and a half later Frank called me. "Could you come and check her out Doc, she still hasn't calved and we might as well do a C-section." So once again, I was off.

After a short discussion and assessment, I cut out two healthy purebred calves and sewed her back up again. The cow likely wouldn't get up for a while so I was off to the barn with the calves and after a drench of colostrum, they were looking like they would be fine.

Two days later Frank called and this time he didn't need me out. The cow had gotten up and was doing fine but she had dried off her milk. He had decided to just bottle feed the calves until another cow came along needing a calf. Frank was happy and after thanking me was off.

I was surprised when the very next day Sunday night Frank called again. "It's the twins now. I think the one has started to suck on the other's navel and started it bleeding. There's blood everywhere and the one calf can't get up and is just stretched out, weak like. Could you come out Doc? I don't want to lose it."

So once again, I was off for the fourth time in a week to the same farm on the same case. The twin calves had indeed been sucking each other's navels and the one calf had sucked so hard that it had caused the little bull calf to bleed out nearly to death. It lay in the straw cold, clammy, white gummed and weak. We ran an old cow into the chute and sucked a liter of blood from her and ran it into the nearby comatose calf. The cow's life-blood did the trick and soon after, I sutured the bleeding navel and the little calf was back on its feet wandering around looking for something to suck on.

Frank was again thankful and half apologetically asked how much all this would cost. I hadn't figured out the bill, but I knew that we were close to a thousand into her and I told him. Frank half smiled and said, "Well it's not like I'm in it to make money anyway… and at least we got two calves and the cow's going to be fine."

I went home happy that at least everything had lived. My happiness however was cut short the next time I ran into Frank three weeks later. It seems that he had had a run of twins after that first set and had farmed out the two we had worked on to a neighbor. The neighbor was in a hurry feeding the one day and instead of bottle feeding them he drenched them and accidentally drowned them both dead. And that was the end of that!

Saturday Night Bath

My wife is forever after me to bath. She is obsessed that I'm going to show up at her place of work, embarrassingly smelling like a dead cow, with feces and blood smeared all over me. Not that I haven't thought about doing that, but I usually try to stay relatively clean… if not for her at least for the paying customers. I knew I was in for it when she started getting after me on Wednesday about a Saturday evening dinner with the teachers at her school. She told me that I had to be off call from 6 to 11 that night and I was going to need a shave, a haircut and a bath and be dressed to the nines for the affair.

All throughout Saturday I was very aware of the engagement and ended the day relatively unscathed fecally and on time. I was proud of myself as I showered and shaved, getting all the hard to get spots even without my Mom's help. I greased my hair up, polished my teeth and slathered on some anti-stink juices, then stood ready and dressed for formal inspection. After passing my wife's stringent and thorough ocular and olfactory going over, we were off to a night with the teachers.

The evening was enjoyable and by midnight we were home and soon asleep. Shortly after I was awakened when my cell phone rang and an anxious farmer asked me to come out to fix a prolapsed uterus. I silently slipped out of bed, leaving my sleeping wife to her dreams. After a quick change into my long johns, jeans, and proper attitude I was in my truck and off. The particular prolapsed uterus was very difficult. I struggled for a long time to get it back where it belonged. I even found my cumbersome obstetric suit to be in the way and had thrown it off to finish the job. By the time I was done I was exhausted and glad to be heading home.

After a quick look in the mirror of my truck to wipe off a few spots of blood from my face and poof up my slicked hair, I was ready for bed. The house was quiet as I returned and without turning on a light I undressed by the door and snuck into bed without waking anyone. As I closed my eyes and fell asleep, the pleasant smell of aftershave mixed with barn smell reminded me of the wonderful disparity of the life I lived.

My wife's screams woke me in the morning and reminded me of the disparity in her life, namely me. When she had gone to sleep, I was a perfectly coiffed and clean man and when she awoke I was covered from my chest to knees in blood. Of course it wasn't my blood but that of the prolapsed uterus, which had wicked through my cloths and dried on my skin without me realizing it. As I explained this to my wife, the terror in her eyes turned to rage and I quickly got out of her pressed sheets before she added my blood to that of the cows.

Calving Tip

The quickest way to stop having calving problems that require a vet is to buy a proper maternity pen and install it inside a cozy barn. This fact has been pressed home time and again but never as clearly as it has applied to Walter Stiebe.

Walter ran about 70 cows and grain farmed about 4,000 acres. He was a year-round hard worker, but grain was king on his farm. His yard boasted some of the nicest, newest tractors and combines. In the winter, some of the best were kept in an immaculate Quonset. If one of his tractors got sick it was driven into a heated shed where it could be attended to in shirtsleeves at any time of the year. His cattle were not so lucky. They were fed good, but roughed the winter on 80 acres of brushless stubble and calved in January in an open-fronted shed. If anything was sick they were driven up the loading chute and off to a side alley that led to a squeeze. The area was exposed to all weather. I've had to preg check and calve cows there in some pretty foul conditions. Walter had an old leaning barn, but it was so filled with cultivator shovels, canvases and sundry items that only a small pen by the door was available for his cattle. It was here that Walter would drag the occasional chilled calf if it was extremely cold outside.

Walter called me on February 18th at 2:06am. "Harv, I'm sorry to get you up, but I've got a heifer calving and it's not going to come out normal. The feet are huge. "I'll be right out," I responded groggily, while slowly getting out of my warm bed.

"Harv, you know it's real cold out. I think its 50-some below with the wind chill," he apologized. "We could do it in the morning if you think it'll be alright," he added. I wanted to agree so I could crawl back into bed, but it was obvious this couldn't wait.

"No we better get her done now while the calf's alive. Maybe you could get her in the barn out of the wind?" I asked hopefully.

There was a pause, then Walter answered, "Yah, I'll just move some stuff around and get things ready for you. See you soon."

The 45 minute drive to the farm passed in a sleepy blur as my headlights cut through the icy night. My truck thermometer said 42 below and it looked like an East wind was flicking snow forebodingly across the road. Walter's outside squeeze C-section side was exposed to the wind and I found myself hoping desperately that he had found room in the old barn.

When I arrived the lights were on in the barn, so I made my way through the maze of equipment to the back where Walter was finishing fluffing some fresh straw in the pen at the back. A C-section can be done anywhere. You could tie up the cow by the head and then apply a side line to prevent her from moving. The little pen would do just fine since there was an exposed timber on the wall that would provide an anchor for the head. The pen sides would finish the job of tying her up. We quickly brought the heifer in, but when we tried to tie her to the barn wall she went slightly berserk. She bucked and pulled at the halter and sent big looping kicks at us whenever we attempted to get more ropes on her. The old barn creaked and almost moved as the heifer tugged and yanked. We decided to let her go and do her outside before she pulled the barn down. We ran her outside and tightened her down in the squeeze where she finally settled down and let us get on with things.

The rodeo action had warmed us both up and we quickly had the calf out, shining and wet in the arctic cold night. Walter dragged the calf into the barn under a heat lamp and I started to close the steaming incision in the heifer's side. My fingers had been fine while I was elbow deep in the cow's warm innards, but now as I attempted the delicate act of threading needle and suturing, the biting cold starting slicing into me. I also noticed Walter turning blue around the lips and starting to hunch up and shiver inside his snow suit. "This is it," Walter shivered, "Next year I'm fixing the barn up and putting a calving pen in there."

"That's all well and good," I thought. "But it didn't make a difference now!" My hands were starting to really freeze up along with the water in my surgical instrument tray. "Walter, I'm going to need some hot water to thaw this out. Do you mind getting some to pour in here?" I numbly asked. Walter jumped at the chance to get to the house and was soon off while promising to be right back. I continued to close the heifer's incision. The cold was making the usually quick procedure painfully slow. After fifteen minutes, Walter returned with a kettle of hot water and quickly poured its steaming comfort into my surgical tray. While warming my fingers, I noticed a hot chocolate moustache on Walter's pink warm upper lip, so I asked him what took so long. He warmly replied that he couldn't find the kettle right away and didn't want to wake his wife to find it. I told him that hot tap water was all we'd need next time. Walter eagerly assured me he could run and get as much hot tap water as we needed.

The water quickly froze and once again, Walter jumped at the chance to return to the house. This time he returned cheerfully with a pint of lukewarm water and what looked like a jam sandwich moustache. My feet had just about turned to ice and the cold had crept into my body chilling me deep to the bones. The lukewarm water barely melted the ice in the tray and did nothing to thaw my almost useless ice block hands. I sent Walter back for more hot water but asked for a gallon this time. After ten minutes, Walter returned impervious to the cold with his neck open and warm cheeks exposed to the biting wind. "I couldn't find a gallon pail," he replied. "Just this one in the fridge and I had to empty it out first." I couldn't see ice cream on his lip, but I'm sure he hadn't emptied it into the garbage.

"Thanks," I mumbled, finding the concept of eating ice-cream a completely alien and absurd notion on this frozen night. I immersed my hand full into the gallon of warmth until I felt I was sufficiently warmed to finish the job and get the heifer back to her calf.

I don't remember much after the last few stitches as my mind was starting to close down because of the cold, but I do remember steering with my elbows during the slow, painful drive way to Saskatoon as the truck's heater slowly pulled the cold from my hands.

Walter was true to his word and the next summer he propped up his barn and moved a calving squeeze inside. Not that it has made any difference to me... it's been five years since that cold night in February and he hasn't had to call me to a calving yet.

A Good Whipping

Jason Weins had a full time job in town but liked to dabble in livestock on his acreage. He always had horses and had most types of stock on his place at one time or another.

Jason had acquired a couple of Charolais-cross cows the previous fall. One was supposed to calve in June (if you could believe the vet that preg checked her), and the other was supposed to be not bred.

Jason had noticed blood on the tail of the bred cow and was worried that she had slipped her calf or the unborn calf was somehow in distress. He called me and after a brief history we decided that the best bet was to check her out and to see what was going on.

I got to the farm by mid-afternoon. Jason had both cows caught in a 40X50 pen. He had never needed a cattle squeeze before, but it would have come in handy now as both cows were anxiously milling about the enclosure. Jason suggested a rope to secure the cattle and as there was no other option available he went off to fetch a couple of lariats.

When Jason returned, we quickly flipped a loop over the head of the pregnant cow. She didn't quite like the feel of things and before Jason could tighten the rope, she had stepped half way through the loop and was caught by the chest. Off she ripped with Jason half running and half falling behind her. She finally slowed down next to a heavy tie which Jason quickly wrapped a dally around. The cow, refreshed by her break, then took off again, causing the rope to come singing and smoking off the tie to crack Jason hard across the upper thighs. He buckled with pain immediately, holding his legs and moaning.

I rushed over to him and I as I got there, he pulled down his pants to examine two angry 6-inch raised welts on his legs. The lesions were painful just to look at, and not knowing what to do to help Jason's situation, I did what all men do when confronted similarly and started laughing. I couldn't help it... It had all happened so quickly and I was so grateful it wasn't me that had been rope whipped, that I kept laughing.

Poor Jason, after his pain subsided he also laughed a little - then we were off to attend to the cow. This time Jason triple looped the rope around a tie and while the cow strained against the rope, I palpated her rectally and found a nice live, healthy calf. I think we thought we had things figured out and we decided to tackle the next cow, but once again the cow snuck through the loop and got hung up in the mid-section.

The second cow was quite worked up and was soon off at a run. I had the end of the rope this time, thinking I'd give Jason a break. As the cow slowed down I triple wrapped the rope around a heavy post and bore down to stop the cow. She slowed down but then switched to bull low gear and digging in, kept pulling against the rope. The rope tightening around her midsection only encouraged her to pull even harder. I was at a right angle to the cow and Jason was behind her when we noticed the nylon lariat start to stretch. Like a 40 pound pike on 10 pound test that old girl pulled and stretched that rope till Jason jumped aside fearing it's snap and yelled to me to let go. I let go of the rope with both hands and as soon as I did, the rope, like a possessed snake going back to hell, burned its way around the tie and whipped me full in the palm of both hands before whooshing back to the cow. I thought both of my hands were broken and I fell to my knees in pain holding my throbbing hands in front of me.

After a few more minutes of excruciating pain and dips into the cold water trough, I realized that nothing was broken and I'd likely survive. Jason stood quietly beside me but I soon knew that the karmic circle of laughter at another's misfortune was complete as he laughed and told me that it looked like we should stop now and not worry about the other cow because we'd both been whipped good.

No Country for Old Men

(Narration from an old retired Saskatchewan farmer)

When I was born in January 1922, the ring around the moon was bright as the July sun and the weather stayed below thirty for three weeks straight. My Dad minded the cows around the clock and feared for the lives of his calves in the cold. He tended them through the night in our tiny mud-planked barn. The small barn couldn't hold more than five at a time so Dad would rotate them day and night to keep their teats from freezing and keep his calves full bellied and warm. That fall he hauled those calves to market where they fetched ten cents a pound and netted himself 36 dollars a head and not a frozen ear amongst them. I figured that if that was now and all things were equal we should get about thirteen hundred per calf in hard cash money.

In the spring we'd sling manure with the hired hand on flat bottom stone boats and hea and haw the horses over still frozen fields, dotting them with muskrat like piles ready to be worked into the ground after the thaw. Ira the hired hand made 2 dollars a day back then and we worked 'cause we knew Dad would hide us if we didn't. Today a young feller who can't even grow hair on his face and ain't never wore skin off his hands won't crawl out of bed for less than two hundred bucks.

Things have changed and the way of doing things has changed but most things have changed for the wrong. It ain't right that a man farming 12 quarters has to send his wife to town to work so as to pay the bills. It ain't normal that his own flesh and blood can't see the rewards of working the land because his old man worked himself raw and never saw a profit. My own boy's boy grew up right and played in the dirt like we all did but he's gone and painted his hair and got a job in the city. He's got himself a high paying job and works real hard from nine 'til five with an hour off for lunch. Hell, we used to rest the horses at nine cause they'd been ploughing since six and if we ever stopped working at four it was 'cause someone died. I know my boy feels like it's his fault that he's got no help and the boy's gone but I don't hold him to blame. These days' things are getting complicated. When Ma goes to the store the crap she brings back don't look like it ever done time on a farm. I don't think most folks know where eggs come from and I don't reckon they can grapple that, that-there calf grazing by the highway is going to give them their T-bone. Every grain of dirt is washed from their fingernails and they can't see behind them far enough to realize their roots are in the land. I'd say most folks are sterilized to the land. And I think that's part of what's wrong with things. We're feeding people here and feeding them good but all they want to think is that, that piece of meat or lump of butter was made in a factory somewhere and presented to them all sanitized and cheap.

Oh hell, I ain't saying it's all bad. The boy'll likely sell the place after I'm gone but then it won't matter none to me will it? And the other day at coffee row it was just like the fifties when land was opening up, up north, and grain was through the roof. We thought we were kings of the world. All the young boys at coffee row the other day, the ones that stayed on the land are riding high with talk of ten dollar wheat. It sure was something for these old eyes to see.

The Summer of Pete's Pet Pig

I occasionally provide veterinary care to pet pigs, but while growing up pigs were for hams, not for pets.

Back then, Dad farrowed out a few sows every year to provide some pork for our freezer and cash for the bills. We would all be involved with slopping and tending the hogs in the barn and I remember the fun we had watching the young pigs growing up, rooting and fighting in the barn yard. As farm kids, we were aware of where bacon came from, so we never got too attached to the hogs… until one day… A large litter was born and Dad brought the runt into the house for the 'boys' to tend. Peter, as the youngest was tasked with the job and soon had the little sow following him around the yard and meeting the school bus like she was a dog and Pete was her master. The little pig was a great pet and we all chased her around and played with her as she grew. She would sleep in the porch and hang around the house all day, never seeming to want to wander back to the barn where the other pigs were.

Pete in particular, became quite attached with the hog and I knew he was worried about her future. Our farm was quite utilitarian where everything served a purpose. A pet pig was cute but cute didn't butter the bread. Had the little pig been a boar the end would have been assured. We hoped, however, that this little pig's gender would save her from a trip to the market.

Dad finally reassured us when he told my brother to reintroduce his pet back to the hog pen so she could be ready for breeding.

The little pig was about two months old and close to 60 pounds. I remember my brother carrying her into the pen and setting her down with 15-20 other similar sized hogs. As we left her there for her first night away from the house she stood on the edge of the pig pen and peeked over grunting at us as if to ask where we were going and who were all these stinky pigs sniffing at her. The next morning before going to school my brother ran out to check on his little pig. The sad look on his face as he returned to the house and started to get ready for school told it all. During the night the other pigs in the pen had badly beat up Pete's pet. She was badly bruised and it appeared that her back was broken.

I didn't have school that day, so I ran to the barn to check things out for myself. Dad had taken her out of the pen and she was resting comfortably by herself eating, drinking and grunting contently as she gurgled the fresh milk and chop Dad had poured into her bowl. "Just leave her there for now and we'll see what she does," Dad told me. I knew that if she didn't get up pretty soon, that would be the end of her and silently prayed for some miracle.

Back on the farm in the old days before Walt Disney, miracles weren't so common and by lunch she still hadn't gotten any better. That's when Dad told me to tell Mom to get the barbeque pit ready and then go ahead and butcher her. I sure wished that I had school that day as I would have traded twelve chapters of trigonometry over butchering Pete's pet pig. Somehow I got the job done and before the bus returned at 4 in the afternoon the little pig was buried under coals slowly roasting for supper. Pete never cried when he found out. I think he knew the reality of things but he couldn't eat a bite. Mom made him his favorite supper instead.

The impact of the summer pig project has lasted throughout the years as even now we cannot barbecue pork without remembering.

Bales for Christmas

The summer of 76 was dry, but the rains came when they had to and we had a good hay crop to take off. All through the long hot days of July my Dad, my six brothers and I baled the hay lands, the sloughs and the ditches with the old New Holland square baler. The crop was thick and regularly plugged the old baler and snapped one cotter pin after another. But as the baler swallowed up the swath, the bale counter counted higher and higher, soon reaching record levels.

We quickly filled the barn loft beetling the heavy green bales up the elevator to the waiting hands of the unlucky stackers in the stifling dusty heat. Then, a new bale yard large enough to handle the bountiful harvest was created and rack by rack and day by day we began constructing a bale stack to rival them all. The stack was built interlocking like Lego and was as solid as the ancient pyramids. Over the course of the haying season the stack grew and grew to 20 bales high at the peak, tapered to shed the rain and snow. We finished the stack in mid-August with some slough hay and a few green feed bales and there she stood... a monstrous monolithic mass of bales reaching for the sky. The stack was a testament to our summer's work and as school started and summer's heat turned to fall's cool, the giant stack reminded us that like good hard-working ants, we were ready for winter.

It was a grey cool day in early November when Mom and Dad decided to go to town and left the kids in charge of my oldest brother, who was out of school at the time. He met me and my other brothers as we got off the bus, with his pellet gun in hand, eager to show us what he had been doing. He had discovered that by cutting down wooden matches and sticking them in the pellet gun, they would go off with a crack and puff of smoke if they were shot against something hard. After a half hour of his firepower demonstration, we were all off to start doing chores and milk the cows, except for my two youngest brothers, who by virtue of their age only had to feed the chickens. My older brothers match demonstration had apparently lit the fires of imagination in their young minds and they grabbed some matches and decided to light a little fire. The wind quickly blew out the matches as they tried to light a pile of grass in the dirt yard... so, what better place to start a fire but in the lee of the giant hay stack...

14 hours later as the firefighters packed their truck and left the farm, all that remained was a half-foot of black volcanic rock-like remnants of the bales. They had not been able to save a single bale.

The loss of the bale stack put the farm in a real financial bind. Neighbors helped a lot and we scavenged as much ditch hay as we could before the snow came, but we were going to be short and had to buy feed. My one brother worked off the farm and contributed his wage to buying hay, but basically every penny that the farm had went into buying bales to get the cows through winter.

It was about mid-December when Mom said that maybe we wouldn't be able to have too much for Christmas. All the kids were disappointed to be sure, but we knew that the cows had to come first and it wasn't like we didn't have anything to eat.

Christmas came and just like Mom said, Santa missed our house except for the few small stocking gifts and a family game or two. We moped around all Christmas holidays and every time we fed the cows old ditch hay or poor quality bought hay we were reminded of what might have been.

The New Year approached and as we prepared for our return to school and the embarrassment of the 'what did you get for Christmas' questions, we got news of a large parcel at the bus station. The parcel was brought home and out of the box, just like Santa's toy bag, flowed gifts for everyone. My bachelor uncle in Vancouver had heard of our misfortune and decided that out of his good fortune he would help us. I still remember those gifts and the joy they brought us that late December evening, a reminder of how blessed we are.

You may be a Saskatchewan Red-Neck if...

1. ...you're using the same needle to vaccinate your cows that your Daddy's Daddy used.

2. ...you like your long acting Liquamycin like your coffee, black and thick.

3. ...you feed your pregnant wife at night to make sure she has the baby during the day.

4. ...you only call the vet out to a calving if the tractor you usually use to pull out the calves doesn't start.

5. ...you paid more for your truck tires than you did for your herd sire.

6. ...talk of castrating calves gets you hungry.

7. ...you've ever called a cow stupid then hit her with a shovel or poked her with a pitchfork.

8. ...you don't feed your dog during calving season 'cause he can live off the dead pile'.

9. ...you bought satellite TV not for the movies but in order to watch 'live cattle auctions'.

10. ...you think blackberries are something that you get from banding yearling bulls.

Lab Tests

Allen Jack's calves were dropping like flies. He was in the middle of calving about one hundred and forty cows and he had already dragged about eight calves to the dead pile. He had another six real sick ones and had treated about twenty more that looked like they might live, but they were real rung out and set back. I talked to him on the phone several times during the week and made a few suggestions as to what he might try… but nothing had really helped.

Allen finally asked me to come out to see if maybe I could find a way to staunch his losses. I knew that Allen's outbreak was related to diarrhea since all the dead calves went through a 12 hour course of foul scours before lying down flat out. He would sometimes be able to treat and save a calf and other times the same treatment would have no effect. I looked at a few real sick calves and took some fecal samples but found nothing enlightening.

We then went to the dead pile and I commenced post mortems on a few of the fresher dead calves. All calves had the same inflamed bowls bursting with putrid bloody fecal matter. The liver and kidneys were spotted with infection and some of the lungs were also inflamed. I took representative samples from about four calves and wrapped them all in plastic bags to send to the lab. (Whenever a deadly agent is running amuck and not responding to traditional therapies, I find it very useful to send samples to the lab so we can identify exactly what we are dealing with.) Allen was hoping for answers as soon as possible and I could understand his anxiety. I could offer him little new information, just the hope that within a few days we'd have results from the lab and we'd know how to treat the problem.

I gave him the standard protocols for dealing with an infection outbreak like this one. I told him to identify any sick calves early and treat any suspicious calves as quickly as possible. I told him to separate all sick calves from the healthy ones and if possible move the healthy ones to fresh ground. I told him to burn the pile of dead calves and clean up any spots where they scoured. He promised he'd keep at it but had no place to move his cattle to - all his pens were full and the pasture was out of the question (it was over a quarter section of land and full of trees - he'd never be able to find a calf if it was sick). Laying all his hopes on the results of those tests, he said he'd tough it out until the results came back from the lab.

I was soon off with the box of assorted intestinal goodies, but was diverted to a number of other calls before I could get the samples into the lab by closing time. "No problems," I thought, "I'll get them to the lab first thing in the morning."

My truck box was heated and my wife has a rule about guts in the refrigerator, so when I got home that evening I removed the samples from the back of the truck and laid them in the driveway. The early spring nights hovered around zero degrees and would be perfect for preserving my samples until the morning.

The phone rang at just after seven the next morning, It was Allen. "I did like you told me," he exclaimed. "I burned that pile of dead calves and cleaned up the yard. Have you heard from the lab yet?"

"No, we won't hear for a while yet," I answered. "It might be a few days yet. Have any more died since yesterday?" I asked.

"No everything's the same but I'll let you know," Allen promised. I was soon out the door ready for a quick stop at the lab when I noticed a bloody bag blowing behind my truck. The box containing about a gallon of miscellaneous calf parts had been ripped open, (likely by a dog) and the entire cache of valuable scientific data was gone. I could have cried as I felt through the empty ripped bags and found nothing but bloody plastic and ripped cardboard.

I was soon back on the phone to Allen and this time got his wife Jill. "Is Allen around? I need to talk to him," I asked.

"No, he's out chasing the cows. They busted out a while ago and have scattered into the bush of the home pasture," Jill answered.
"Well get him to call me when he is in please. I have to talk to him," I replied.

In a couple of hours a dejected Allen called. "All the cows are out and there's no way I can get them back. I guess I'll have to leave them there and try and catch the sick ones if I have to. Did you get some results?" he queried anxiously. I apologetically told him what had happened and that with no additional calves available we'd have to wait for the next one to die. "Well that won't be long," a disappointed Allen answered. "I'll let you know as soon as the next one dies."

After two days with no calls from Allen, I decided to check in with him, thinking maybe he had given up on me after my mishap and gone elsewhere for help. I was pleasantly surprised when Allen explained happily that nothing had died since we last talked. In fact, he never lost another calf to the diarrhea and it seemed that the change in the ground had done a world of good for the rest of his calves.

We never found out exactly what agent was at play in Allen's yard, but about a day later my neighbor told me that his dog had thrown up the oddest assortment of things on his living room floor and had been passing some of the foulest gas he'd ever smelt. So, in the end, I guess Allen did get his Lab(rador) test run, and free of charge to boot.

Jessie the Farm Dog

Jessie epitomized everything you wanted in a good farm dog. He was good with cows, never in the way, but always there when you needed him to turn a cow or chase a calf. He was tough and never daunted by any kind of weather. His scruffy black and white coat was matted and dirty. He was faithful and stayed by John's side as he did chores and checked cows. Jessie had iron guts. I witnessed him eating everything including a day old dead gopher. All in all, Jessie was the type of dog every cattle ranch needed.

Jessie's only drawback was that he was a shih tzu. That's right... Jessie was a twenty pound, sit-in-your lap and share your tea and crumpets shih tzu. Somewhere along the line Jessie was never told that he shouldn't be wandering around in corrals or digging gophers. But I imagine, if someone had told him that, it wouldn't have made any difference.

I got to know Jessie quite well one winter as misfortune after misfortune befell his owner and ultimately Jessie himself. John calved from January to March and this particular year, nothing went right from start to finish. Twins were twisted, calves were big and stuck, uteruses protruded and heifers played-out while calving, leaving big hip-locked calves to die in the cold.

Then the final icing on the cake... as calving season petered out, calves began dying from viral diarrhea. Some weekends it felt as if I lived at John's - running IV's and administering last rites. John had rigged a temporary scour ward inside his barn where we could connect a number of calves to IV solution sets underneath a bank of heat lamps. Throughout all this, little, scruffy Jessie acted as a wet nurse and assistant to me and the calves. Jessie was never underfoot but always around to wash the sick calves faces as they lay in the straw or to offer his furry yoda-like head for me to scratch and warm my fingers on.

Through this grim season John and Jessie never wavered emotionally. Every time I drove into their yard John would greet me with a resigned smile and friendly hello while Jessie would wag his tail and greet me with a slobbery lick to the boot. I asked John once about his optimism in the face of such a horrible winter and he answered that 'it is what it is' and that there was 'no worries, things would work out'. I knew that John was a religious man and I knew that his faith played a part in his ability to deal with things. This impressed me.

I really wanted things to improve for John and his young family and after about a week of not hearing from him, I thought we had maybe turned the corner. Then, a 10pm call changed that. It was John apologizing for calling on a late, snowy night but another calf needed IV'ing. I was in the truck and on the road shortly, but the heavy snow delayed my arrival. As I pulled beside the barn, John and little Jessie, buried to the chest in snow, stood waiting for me. We knew the routine and within half an hour the calf was perking up as the warm fluids ran into his veins. John, Jessie and I sat contently in the straw around the calf while the snow fell silently outside. I asked John how things were going. In his usual, optimistic tone, he replied that he thought things were coming along. Most of the calves were through the susceptible age where the highest death loss had occurred and he was pretty well done calving. I loaded up my truck, happy that finally the sad saga at John's was coming to a close. Waving good-bye to John and Jessie I pulled away from the barn, but got half stuck trying to do a U-turn in the yard. John came to the window and said that I'd likely need to back up in my tracks as the snow was too deep to turn around ahead. The snow was falling quite heavily and in the dark I couldn't see very well but by straightening the wheels I was able to readily back out. I was soon on the highway and home.

I called John later the next day to ask how the calf was doing. He told me that the calf was doing well and he was going to pull the IV soon. I was glad for him and didn't need to talk to him for a while. It was about two weeks later when John called with a simple question concerning one of his bulls. In the course of the conversation John told me (half apologetically) that I had run over and killed Jessie on the last snowy night I had been at his place. "NO!" I thought to myself, "How was that possible?" John explained that when I had backed out Jessie couldn't get out of the truck rut and I had run him over. John had seen it happen but couldn't do a thing to prevent it and Jessie had died seconds after being run over. I apologized, feeling genuinely sorry for the loss and anguish that I had caused. John never skipped a beat.

He quickly responded on the phone, "No worries Harv, it is what it is."

Close Call at the Calving

The wildest cow I ever calved out was a dirty, old, goggle eyed crossbred owned by Murray Eiker. Murray didn't do much with his cattle, he calved year round and for the most part the cattle looked after themselves.

The night he called me out was a rare one and as I arrived at his yard, I thought I might be in for a treat. The cow in question had started to mess around in the early morning and in keeping with Murray's cavalier attitude, he hadn't worried about her until after supper. At that time, he noticed a tiny tip of a tail protruding from her. By the time I arrived, he had enticed the cow into the barn and as I got out of the truck I could see him standing by the barn door. "Hey, Doc," he greeted me. "Glad you came, I've got her in the barn for you."

As I started to open the barn door, Murray quickly pushed it closed saying, "I wouldn't go in right yet, I think she's gone crazy. She almost killed me and she is charging anything that moves."

As if to prove Murray's point, the cow nosed up to the closed door, and snorted and gurgled with rage.

Inside Murray's barn was a 20' X 30' open area with a few part walls extending from the outside. There were no pens and it was dimly lit by two small bulbs that hung from the roof. On one side of the barn a ladder on the wall led to a hayloft. A door at either end accessed the barn. So, it was decided that Murray would distract the cow at the far door while I made a dash for the ladder to the loft. From that point I would attempt to rope the cow and secure her.

Just as planned the cow responded to Murray's enticement and went snorting over to the other end of the barn. I quietly opened the door and raced to the ladder. The cow somehow sensed my presence as soon as I entered the barn and I barely made the ladder as she chased me 'bear' like up the ladder, swiping at my legs as I climbed higher. Dropping a loop on her head was easy as she snorted and bellowed beneath me. I dallied the end of the rope to one of the huge 6X6 uprights that I could reach from the ladder, then called for Murray to come in. As soon as the cow saw Murray, she turned and drove hard towards him stopping short like a junkyard dog on a leash when the rope tightened. She then took to pulling and bucking, slamming into the barn as she strained against the rope. Eventually she played out and choked herself down to the ground where she lay gasping and bug-eyed, oblivious to our presence. Murray quickly threw a rope around her back feet and trussed her up. I jumped down from my safe perch and grabbed my calving kit to work on her. With my hand inside her, she concentrated on straining and pushing and I soon had a dead calf delivered. I cautiously gave the cranky cow her meds where she lay, then took my equipment out to the truck.

Murray was standing by the ropes when he asked me to give him a hand untying her. I said that if he minded the hind ropes, I would slop the head rope off, and then we'd loosen the hind ropes and let her figure her way out herself. The cow lay totally exhausted and spent as I loosened the rope from the post and quietly went up to her to remove the loop from her neck. My gentle touch to her neck was all it took to wake the dead and with a huge lunge she was up and after me. The rope around her feet momentarily slowed her down, just enough for me to jump away and flee to the closest wall only to find myself in a corner with no escape, the bellering cow bearing down on me. My dally to the post was rapidly unraveling as I dropped to a fetal position to take the blow I was sure was coming. Then, out of the corner of my eye, I saw Murray grab the last foot of the flying end of the rope and snub her up about two feet from my crouched body. The cow once again choked herself down and I took the opportunity to escape on wobbly legs. Outside and cleaning up by the truck, I asked Murray what he would have done if he hadn't been able to stop the cow and she had got me. He replied, "Oh we don't get much cell coverage out here, so I'd have had to go up to the house to call for some help."

The Big Red Bull

I was conducting an open-air c-section at about 1 in the morning when the talk turned to long-haul trucking (my assisting farmer was one in his spare time). It was biting cold. I was thankful for the chance to converse to keep my frozen face from falling off. We talked about the joys of driving on winter roads and he shared stories of his many experiences. Talks eventually turned to tricks to stay awake on overnight trips. I shared with him my reliance on coffee and how caffeine would keep me awake. I always grab a quick cup of java for late night calls and find it perks me up and gets me through when I don't get much sleep. It turned out my assistant had just started marketing a super-duper, stay awake juice. He'd been peddling it to his fellow truckers. He swore by it and as I finished the C-sections, he offered me a couple of promotional cans to try out. (This was about five years before the present rush of energizing, caffeine-laden drinks hit the stores. I was intrigued by the thought of coffee in a can.)

It was only 20 minutes to my warm bed, so I thought I'd save my free samples until I really needed them. Just as I crawled exhausted into my bed the phone rang - someone needed assistance for a calving one hour away. I was back in my truck, but not before chugging down a can of the new prep juice (I left my coffee mug at home). A mere 15 minutes into my drive, with the lights of Saskatoon still in my rear view mirror, I felt myself dozing off. I reached for my second can and quickly downed it. The sugary elixir tasted good and I was bright and awake for about five minutes before I once again felt the 3am cobwebs filling my head. I cranked the window, cranked Art Bell, and cranked my eyelids wide open and eventually got to the farm.

The calving was uneventful and I was soon on my way home. The return drive was even more of a chore than it was getting there. I was now extremely tired and cursing myself for not bringing along some coffee, instead of trusting the cans, which likely contained some kind of sleeping agent.

After using all the tricks in the book to stay awake including forcing myself to eat the old cheesy that was stuck between the seats, I finally arrived home and plunked, totally exhausted into my own warm bed. That's when someone turned the lights on in my head. Every creak of the bed, drip of water, tread of cat become like a pounding in my brain. Every crack in the ceiling, swirl of paint on the wall, minute item on the dresser jumped out at me like the brightest July afternoon. My caffeine-laden blood roared like rapids through my body. Although I thought that at 5:30 in the morning it would be a good idea to have a nap, it appeared that it simply was not going to happen. The rush stayed with me until my alarm rang at seven and throughout the day as I whipped through my calls. Finally at about eight that evening, the train stopped and I landed hard. I could barely hold my eyes open and prayed for no calls as I sank deep into sleep swearing I would never ride the big red bull again.

Out with the Garbage

It was around midnight and I was asleep when the phone rang. It was Debbie. I could hear loud hip-hop music and partying going on in the background. "It's Sugar, she's having her babies and we are right in the middle of our kid's sixteenth birthday party and I don't know what to do," she sobbed into the phone. Debbie was a mother of three teenagers. She also had three dogs - two small and one large. Sugar was a tiny Maltese who was accidentally bred as a teenager to a much larger yorkie male. Sugar's belly had been expanding exponentially for the last three weeks and now it looked like things were ready to pop. I told Debbie I would be over and quickly drove to her house.

When I arrived, the house looked like anything but a maternity ward. Loud music thumped through the house and kids joked and danced around in the dim shadows. Debbie thanked me for coming, and then took me to a back bedroom where Sugar lay on her little bed straining and looking for help. A group of teenagers huddled wet-eyed and mascara streaked around the little dog. It was a stark contrast to the oblivious, joyful teens in the adjacent rooms as they looked pleadingly to me for help. A quick digital exam revealed a large, likely dead pup at the pelvic inlet with a Riders chance in BC of getting out naturally. I told Debbie the unfortunate news that Sugar would need a c-section.

I grabbed Sugar and left a much subdued group with a promise to call as soon as I was finished. I would be flying solo for this surgery as Sugar was very manageable and I didn't think I needed to call in anyone else for help at this late hour. Things went well and I quickly had Sugar anesthetized and on the surgery table with her swollen abdomen waiting my scalpels touch to release its burden of pups. The expected pups turned out to be two massive ones, one in each horn. Their removal from the stretched uterus was difficult and as each pup came forth, their lifeless body was laid on a towel, where I attempted to resuscitate it. I worked for a few minutes on each pup, injecting them with stimulants, attempting to start their hearts and get them breathing. It appeared that the prolonged stress of whelping, coupled with the anesthetics used to sedate Sugar had killed the pups in the uterus. I lay the pups in a box with the other surgical garbage and returned to sew up Sugar.

Ten minutes later I was just starting to close the abdomen when I glanced over to the garbage box. I thought I saw the blood soaked gauze move. It was now close to 2am and the clinic was dark and spookily quiet. I thought that my tired mind was seeing things. But there it was again, the same movement! I quickly shed my surgical gloves and dug into the refuse box. I searched for what was alive in there. I came to the dead pups and as I touched the still bodies they open mouth gasped. They were alive! I grasped each pup in turn and gently CPR'ed them until they miraculously started breathing regularly and had regained a steady heart rate. I was overjoyed at this turn of good fortune and happily returned to Sugar and finished suturing her up

Sugar woke up soon after I completed the surgery and she immediately, albeit groggily started licking her pups. The pups were becoming more and more animated by the minute and you soon couldn't tell that I had declared them clinically dead and thrown them in the garbage a scant hour ago. I phoned Debbie expecting to wake her up but instead was greeted by the same music and party noise I had heard earlier. I told her the good news and she was ecstatic and eager to get Sugar and the pups back-tonight if at all possible. I thought to myself that if I had just been given a C-section, the last place I'd want to be would be in a house full of teenagers and pounding music. I told Debbie I'd drop her off as soon as I could in the morning.

I waited until around ten the next morning before I called. This time I got Debbie out of bed. She answered gravelly and told me that I could bring Sugar and the pups over right away. I drove over to Debbie's and she let me into her house blaming the kid's party for the mess. Kids were sprawled and sleeping wherever they fell amongst the discarded garbage and bottles of last night's party and as I surveyed the scene I told her not to worry, the pups would feel right at home.

Batting 500

The late winter night started with a ten o'clock call to a calving out in the Borden area. The night was mild, loaded with promise of spring and the release from the frosty grip of winter. I was well rested and full of energy, ready for whatever the night would bring.

I arrived at the farm in good time and was led to a dark corner in the barn, where a cow was caught in a squeeze. She was standing quietly and did not look like a cow with calving problems. "She's been off most of the day, so I finally ran her in and checked her out. When I felt a tail, I called you right away." I was told.

I quickly gloved up and got ready to address the situation. After a quick palpation, I determined it was a breach, (the calf was backwards and the feet were down). After injecting her to stop her straining and relax the uterus, I went back inside and also discovered that the calf had wrapped its umbilical cord around its hind leg. The stakes had been raised for the little calf, as his life now depended on getting his legs up and out without breaking his cord and killing him. After a few minutes of manipulation I was able to slip his leg out of his pulsating, life giving cord. Within a few more minutes, we had him on the ground, wet and vigorously shaking his head oblivious to his close call.

I left the farm feeling quite good inside, as it always does after a successful calving. I'd just settled in for the drive home when my phone rang "Are you close by? I just pulled a big calf from a cow and now her calf bed is out," Joe from Asquith anxiously asked.

"I'm not far Joe," I answered. "I should be there in 25 minutes." And I was off to the next one, speeding down the dark road.

I was just climbing up the other side of the Borden Bridge, my old Ford Ranger pulling against gravity, when out of nowhere a whitetail doe struck the corner of my truck and flopped dead in the ditch. I stopped to make sure she was dead and determined that my truck was road worthy. Then, I was off again.

The prolapse was one of the worst I'd seen and for a while I wondered if we'd ever get the large, swollen, blood-filled organ back in before the cow died. A full 30% or more of cows like her die. But she hung in there and even stood up and licked her big calf after we were done replacing the uterus.

I was off once again, heading home and feeling alright at another success, when a skunk waddled out of the ditch and onto the road where I promptly ran him over. The pungent skunk odor was wafting into the truck when the phone rang. This time, it was Keith from Donovan. "Sorry to wake you Harv, but we got a heifer calving and I think it's too big. Can you make it out?" "No problem! I'm on the road. I'll be there right away." I was soon pulling into the yard where Keith and his brother John met me holding their noses at the skunk stink emanating from my truck. "She's this way, but I think the calf's dead- it's all swollen up.

I got to the heifer and noticed two large feet protruding about a foot from the heifer and a nose with a hugely swollen tongue peeking out at us. I gloved up and checked her out, deciding that the calf should fit if we lubed her up and slowly pulled it out. The brothers had tried before they'd called, but had hesitated, scared by their lack of progress and at the size of the feet. I lubed up the calf and after a few minutes of hard pulling he was on the ground and, surprise-surprise, alive, swollen, but alive! I left the boys with some meds to get the swelling out of the head and instructions to tube-feed the calf because he wouldn't be able to suck.

I was soon on my way home, happy that we had got the calf out alive without a C-section. Ten minutes into the ride home a big jack rabbit with a death wish decided to run onto the road, ending his life with a thud.

The last 30 minutes of the ride home were uneventful and as I crawled into my bed, I thought back on the night that I just had. Three potentially dire situations had wondrously turned out just fine, but the high road kill count had ruined my perfect game.

Compound Grief

Ted called about mid-morning while I was just starting surgery on a dog. He wanted to know what he should do about his daughter's old cow. The cow was about sixteen and had calved two weeks prior. She had since developed a mastitis that developed into a full blown gangrenous foul infection in two of her quarters and now the old cow was depressed, off feed and breathing heavily. I told Ted that it didn't sound very encouraging, but he should try to get some antibiotics into her and keep her cool until I could get there.

It was midafternoon before I could break away. As I pulled into the yard, I could see that I was too late as the cow lay in the barnyard with feet to the sky. Ted morosely walked towards me with his new pup Jep bouncing around at his feet. He told me the cow laid down and died about a half an hour after we had spoken. He explained that it wouldn't have been so hard except that it was his daughter's pet cow that was such a quiet friendly thing – the whole family would be distraught over her death. In fact, Ted had called both his wife at work and his daughter at school that morning to tell them of the cow's declining condition. His disclosure had led to many tears on the phone and this reassurance of hope for the cow. Ted was now dreading the return of his family when he would be faced at having to break the bad news. We decided to take a look at the cow and after a cursory post-mortem determined that the gangrenous mastitis had led to a toxic condition, which inevitably killed her. There was little that could have been done.

Ted, the bouncing dog Jep and I returned to my truck just as the school bus followed by his wife's car pulled into the yard. Ted suggested that I sneak out to avoid the inevitable tears. I agreed, knowing that this was a family time and nothing I could say could help the situation.

As I started down the lane, I could see Ted's daughter running towards the dead cow, tears coursing down her face – her mother following close behind her. I thought to myself that this is one of the sad facts of life that farm folks have to face, when out of my rear view window I saw Jep run out of the ditch and promptly get run over by my rear tire. I quickly stopped and jumped out of the truck. Ted and his family had witnessed the accident and were now running towards what looked like a stone dead Jep lying on the road. We all arrived together and as the tears and wails poured fourth I started CPR on the little pup. After a few manipulations, Jep thankfully responded and began having seizures. Mouthing apologies, I ran back to the truck and got some meds to stabilize the pup. He slowly recovered and was soon wobbling around after being knocked out and crushed over the hips.

After many more apologies for the dog and condolences for the cow, I slowly left the yard, driving carefully so as to avoid adding more to their grief.

Muddy Needles

What a year for mud and prolapsing uteruses. A uterus or calf bed is meant to be on the inside, but occasionally it follows the calf out of the cow and causes somewhat of a medical emergency. Large blood vessels inundate the organ and can burst, causing the cow to either die from loss of blood or go into deadly shock from the pain and distress.

I got a call at about midnight on a clear, bright spring night to attend a prolapsed uterus at Mcashew's yard. Gord Mcashew and his two boys raised dogs and cows and had an extremely busy yard with machinery, piles of lumber and junk throughout. In the center of this was a 40' x 40' pen with a few round bale feeders and twenty or thirty cows waiting to calve. The pen was deep with mud and puddles except for one mound of straw where most of the cows congregated like refugees on a tiny overcrowded island. The cow that needed attention on this night had lain tight against a bale feeder where she calved, then promptly prolapsed.

Gord Mcashew led me through the sucking mud with this tiny dim flashlight barely showing the way. The cow lay on her side and breathed deeply as she stared at us. The calf was alive and covered in mud as he flopped for footing and tried to stand. One of the Mcashew boys dragged the calf over to the bedding pack, forcing a couple of cows into the mud to make room. The cow's calf bed was half submerged in the mud and manure, so I got the boys to pull the cow up on her sternum to better expose the uterus and facilitate its return to its proper location. The cow preferred to lie on her side, so it was quite a struggle to keep her sitting up. The Mcashews were big strong men and between the three of them they somehow pushed her away from the feeder allowing me to attend to the uterus. After a quick wash to remove some of the dirt from the hopelessly filthy uterus, I started to push it back in. "Don't you think you should wash it some more?" Gord asked. "I don't want her getting an infection from all the manure." "Well, she sure might get an infection," I replied. "But it's more important to get this back in and keep her from damaging it worse than it is." "I'll wash it when it's gone back in," I added, thinking that with this muck in her she'd be extremely lucky not to get an infection.

After about fifteen minutes of struggle, everything was back in place. With an exclamation of "It's in!" the Mcashews stood up en-mass and the cow promptly flopped to her side.

Once a uterus is replaced it is important to sew up the cow to prevent it from coming out again. The needle of choice is a primitive weapon about 12 inches long and as thick as a pencil. It is razor sharp at one end and allows you to pass a string through the cow to keep things in place.

The cow was now lying on her side and I thought that I could wend the needle in place and get her sewn up without moving her. The only problem was that she was deep in the mud. I would have to find and drive the needle through, in the dark, with mud and greasy manure all over my partly numb and cold hands. I maneuvered the big needle as best I could with one hand. The other hand held the cows hide ready for the needle. With an awkward push I drove the needle through the correct spot and right through the palm of my hand. I didn't realize what I had done until I attempted to pull my hand away from the needle… and it stuck. There was no pain thanks to the semi-numbness of my cold hands and I removed the needle with one quick pull and re-sewed her without poking myself again. In the darkness I had driven the dirty shaft through my hand without the Mcashews noticing. As I finished, Gord asked me to give her a double dose of penicillin "Because there's something in this dirt that sure kills 'em if they get infected."

Those words hung my head as I headed home. As the numbness left my hand it was replaced by a sharp pain, so I decided to stop and doctor myself. I squirted long-acting penicillin in and around the wound, wrapping it tight with tape until I could get to a real doctor the next day. I'm grateful to say both the cow and I survived without getting an infection!

The Luckiest Cow in the West

Old Frank Makurik had the fattest cows I have ever seen. Frank was a bachelor who farmed in the woods and kept 20 of the most fortunate cows in Western Canada. These cows never saw a day that the food bunk wasn't full or the grass wasn't belly deep. They never felt the cold of the night in winter or summer as each evening Frank would call his cows home and tie them into the old log barns. There they would be hand fed grain and hay while their calves slept scattered in the barn.

Frank didn't like to sell his cows, but once he had to sell a six year old opened heifer when she still hadn't calved. That heifer topped the scales at over 1800 pounds. Frank's love of his cows allowed him to call the vet at a moment's difficulty and I ended up running to his place a disproportionate amount of times for the number of cows he kept. One time Frank phoned and in his old country accent asked, "You come see my cows I vant you to look at foot where she have hard time valking".

When I arrived Frank had the old cow in a stall where she stood face buried in the nicest green hay you could imagine. Frank pointed out the foot that was sore and I gently touched it and was promptly booted. He said smiling "Vatch her, she likes to kick". I then stepped back and watched the old cow stand firmly on the sore leg. I couldn't see any swelling or signs of footrot. When I asked Frank how she walked he said, "Oh, she good valking but every vants in a vile she lift the leg like it sore, maybe you should tie up one leg and see for abscess". With Frank, I always did like he said, even though this case wasn't looking much like an abscess but more like an overweight cow with mild joint arthritis.

I thought that it wouldn't hurt to check, so I got my ropes and hoof trimmer. In between wild reaching kicks I was able to catch and tie the affected hoof. You would think that a grossly overweight senior citizen cow with one foot stretched to the roof would relax and take her medicine, but not this one. She struggled mightily, jumping around, pulling her sore foot while I scraped and finally determined that the foot was abscess free. Just as I finished and was about to untie her, she gave her gargantuan leap and twisted and landed thunderously with her full weight on her shoulder. I quickly untied her whereby she calmly placed her feet under her and rose regally in her stall. I noticed that she was now favoring the front leg that she had landed on, so I gave her a shot of pain killers and told Frank that the cow might be sore for a few days after her shenanigans. Frank replied, "don't worry I keep cow in barn and make sure she okay before letting out". With that, I was quickly off, hoping that things would work out for the old cow.

Frank called two days later to tell me "You fix that leg. Good on the hind, but now seem like she got it in the front leg. I going to keep an eye on her and maybe she get better." I told him that it was likely from the fall in the barn but Frank answered, "No, it's same as before. I t'ink infection gone from hind to front but I keep good eye on her and she going to be okay".

It was about a month later and I was called back to Frank's for an unrelated call. When I asked how the old cow was doing, Frank replied, "Oh she still sore. Can't walk, but I keep her separate and she doing fine. You come see." With that he took me behind the barn. If the main herd was enjoying 5 star comforts, this cow was enjoying ten stars. The old cow stood chewing her cud by herself in the belly high grass of her exclusive ten acre resort. A small shed was thickly bedded and a trough of remnants of this morning's barley sat in front of it. The cow gazed at me from her luxurious stupor and I think she winked at me acknowledging my part of her lifestyle upgrade.

Spring Rodeo

It was late March around 10pm when Evan called and said he had a cow with a big calf. It looked like she would need a C-Section. I jumped in my truck and after about an hour pulled into his yard. Evan's yard was well lit and had a large pen with a corner catch pen leading to a runway with a squeeze at the end. From my truck I could see Evan chasing and being chased by a big Simmental-cross cow as he tried to work her into the chute system. This old girl was quite worked up and was coming quite close to ramming Evan who was only able to stay safe by climbing the fence as she charged. I hollered at Evan to wait a minute and I'd give him a hand.

Sometimes two heads are better than one, but this time my arrival only served to escalate the cow's anger. She raced back and forth between Evan and I and after about 30 minutes of no progress, Evan announced that he would lead her to the crowding tub if I could shut the door behind her. Evan was in his fifties and I don't think I've ever seen him run, but if he was willing to risk his neck, who was I to disagree? So, while I occupied the cow's attention at the fence, Evan snuck down into the pen and into the crowding tub gate. Just like Evan had planned, the old cow spotted him and gave chase. Evan just made it out the other side of the crowding pen ahead of the cow and I slammed the gate locking her in. After some further prodding we finally got her into the squeeze and I examined her, confirming a large live calf and that we needed to do a C-Section.

Evan was off to get lights and water and I commenced to prepare her for surgery. The cow remained hyper-agitated in the shoot and I decided to blind fold her to calm her down. I wrapped a pair of coveralls around her head and tightly secured it under her jaw. The cow again took exception to the blind fold and tossed her head to and fro while I clipped and froze her side. Evan had returned with the water and light and I started to wash the cow's side. I was about to suggest a halter to stop her from tossing her head around, when she somehow lifted her head and popped open the gate. In a flash she was back in the yard from which we had just driven her. This time, twice as cranky and blind.

The rodeo started all over again. This time the cow would charge at our voices, crashing into the railing coming quite close to getting a hold of us a few times. After 30 minutes of this, Evan suggested the same trick as before – this time using sound as a lure. I think that this night, the calving gods where with us as the cow responded to Evan's banging in the crowding tub and charged in where we caught her again. We quickly haltered her head down and finally had her where we wanted her.

An hour and a half later, we had a healthy calf on the ground and I was busy sewing up the cow's side. We dragged the calf over into some straw in front of the cow and I removed her blind fold, and then cautiously opened the head gate expecting the cow to explode out looking for a fight. Instead she calmly stepped through the opening, almost mindful of her fresh stitches and walked over to her calf where she started to lick it. She never paid any attention to us and you could have sworn she was a milk cow standing so peacefully there. I guess she was just in the mood for a little midnight rodeo at our expense.

End of the Road

Dr. Wally Kononoff was a profound influence through the majority of my veterinary career. He instilled in me early on many of the requirements of being a good veterinarian and a good businessman. When I started working with Dr. K, we worked side by side and shared work and call. Stats tell you that the average career for a large animal veterinarian doing traditional practice is just over 10 years. Cold, wet work takes a toll on a man's body and as Dr. K approached his 30th year in the business, we hired an associate and Dr. K started to slow down and transition the business to me.

As time went by Dr. K did less physical work and was involved more with management and consultation. He would occasionally help out if we were swamped and couldn't attend an emergency. Dr. K would never turn down a request regardless of the time or type of call. It was a mantra he had instilled into me early in my career both as a professional responsibility and as a sound business philosophy.

One bright April Tuesday, loaded with a typical mixed bag of farm calls, we were slammed with a rush of emergencies. I was heading for a colic horse after finishing a prolapsed uterus when the office called about a backwards calving west of town. No one was remotely close or going to be close so Dr. K was suggested and called. He was soon on his way as he still maintained his work truck in constant readiness. I was completely reassured and knew that a backwards calving would be no problem for Dr. K, as he had done many in his career and taught me the proper approach to a difficult calving.

As I carried on to my emergency, the clinic called with yet another emergency. This time it was another cow having trouble calving, but the feet were showing. The call was in the vicinity of where Dr. K was, so a message was dispatched to him after his first call. Dr. K's first calving turned out to be a full breach, meaning butt first and feet down. This is an extremely difficult presentation, and after a prolonged struggle Dr. K got the calf out. The second calving was a normal presentation but two days dead and stinking to high heaven.

Six hours later Dr. K was done both calls and phoned me while motoring back to Saskatoon, tired and foul smelling. He said in an almost apologetic tone that maybe he wouldn't do too many more jobs like that, and that he might have to hang up his chains as he was sore. Years of unrestricted practice and self-sacrifice had taken its toll and Dr. K was getting out while he still could. He continues to help out to this day and is a mentor and a source of support whenever I need him, but is also able to spend quality time with his family.